With Eyes of Wonder Series 1

DISCOVER CALIFORNIA WILDFLOWERS

MaryRuth Casebeer

Illustrated by Peggy Edwards-Carkeet

HOOKER PRESS
Sonora, California

With Eyes of Wonder Series, Vol. 1 *Discover California Wildflowers*. Copyright © 1999 by MaryRuth Casebeer. All rights reserved. Except as noted below, no part of this book may be reproduced or transmitted in any form or by any means, electronic or mechanical, including photocopying, recording, or by an information storage and retrieval system—except by a reviewer who may quote brief passages in a review to be printed in a magazine or newspaper—without permission in writing from the publisher. For information, contact HOOKER PRESS—nature books for children, P.O. Box 3957, Sonora, CA 95370-9165. First printing September, 1998. Second printing November, 1998.

FOR CLASSROOM TEACHERS ONLY: Illustrations may be reproduced free and without special permission to prepare booklets for use in wildflower field studies for elementary and secondary students. Please include a credit line in booklets indicating the title of the book, the artist, and publisher.

Publisher's Cataloging-in-Publication
(Provided by Quality Books, Inc.)

Casebeer, MaryRuth.
    Discover California wildflowers / MaryRuth Casebeer ; illustrated by Peggy Edwards-Carkeet. -- 1st ed.
    p. cm. -- (With eyes of wonder series ; no. 1)
    Includes bibliographical references and index.
    Preassigned LCCN: 98-93219
    ISBN: 0-9665463-0-X

    1. Wild flowers--California. 2. Wild flowers--California--Folklore. 3. Wild plants, Edible--California. 4. Medicinal plants--California. I. Edwards-Carkeet, Peggy. II. Title.

QK149.C37 1998   582.13'09794
                         QBI98-910

582.13

For the Blazing Stars, Brent and Tristan; the Woodland Stars, Lili, Ben, and Emily; and all the children who have learned to love, or will learn to love, the wildflowers of California.

The author wishes to thank several people who contributed their considerable expertise to the successful completion of this book. Thanks to Cordelia Lawton of the Iowa Writers' Workshop for her critical, yet inspiring, editing; to Carol Bartholomew for her sharp proofreading skills and her friendship; to Susanne Nelson for editing the final draft and making pertinent suggestions for accuracy and clarification, both done in a caring way, and for her computer and graphic arts skills; and to my illustrator, Peggy Edwards-Carkeet, another wildflower friend, for her help in making our dream wildflower book become a reality.

Cover design and book production by Dave Bonnot of Columbine Design.

To order additional copies of *Discover California Wildflowers* from the publisher, write:

Hooker Press—nature books for children
P.O. Box 3957
Sonora, CA 95370-9165

Flower Parts and Flower Arrangement on Stems

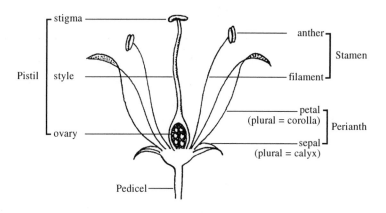

FLOWER PARTS

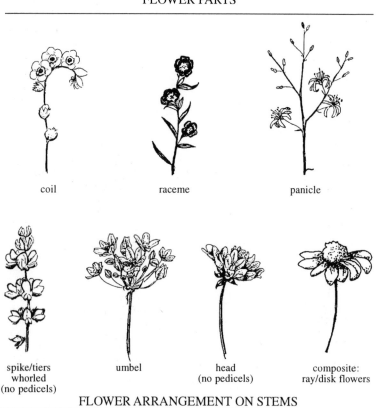

coil   raceme   panicle

spike/tiers   umbel   head   composite:
whorled   (no pedicels)   ray/disk flowers
(no pedicels)

FLOWER ARRANGEMENT ON STEMS

Leaf Shapes and Leaf Arrangement on Stems

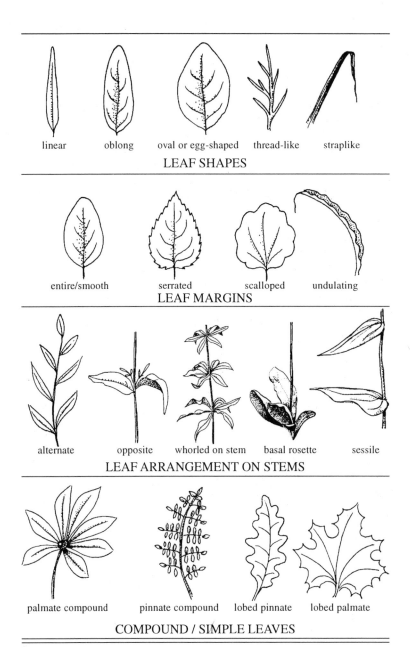

linear   oblong   oval or egg-shaped   thread-like   straplike

LEAF SHAPES

entire/smooth   serrated   scalloped   undulating

LEAF MARGINS

alternate   opposite   whorled on stem   basal rosette   sessile

LEAF ARRANGEMENT ON STEMS

palmate compound   pinnate compound   lobed pinnate   lobed palmate

COMPOUND / SIMPLE LEAVES

ABOUT THE AUTHOR

MaryRuth Casebeer has had a lifelong love of plants, especially wildflowers, and, over the years, has enjoyed sharing her knowledge of California native plants with young people. After retiring as a nutritionist, she organized and implemented the Project Wild Environmental Education program, in conjunction with Senior-Youth Partnership, at Curtis Creek Elementary School near Standard, California. Aside from daily environmental lessons, some of the highlights of the program included: visiting several natural wildflower areas; planting California native conifers in the forest, with follow-up site studies; propagating California native annuals, perennials, shrubs, and trees; establishing a school garden which produced bedding plants for sale, plus vegetables for sampling; and, recycling and composting of the school cafeteria food garbage.

A charter member of the Sierra Foothills Chapter of the California Native Plant Society, she held local art poster contests for elementary school children and, with another chapter member, developed a slide show for use in schools. Additionally, MaryRuth authored several of the articles about California native plants in the Chapter booklets, *Speaking for the Plants, Vols. I and II.* She regularly contributes to the chapter's newsletter, *The Shooting Star,* and to her local newspaper, *The Union Democrat.*

With financial backing from the Sierra Foothills Chapter, MaryRuth initiated a program to give awards to students at the Science Fairs in Calaveras, Mariposa, and Tuolumne counties. Furthermore, through her efforts, books on botany, horticulture, natural history, and California native plants have been placed in forty schools, grades five through eight, in the above-mentioned counties, as well as Amador County—those counties which encompass the geographic area of the Sierra Foothills Chapter.

MaryRuth lives near Sonora, California, within an hour's drive of some of the most fabulous wildflower "gardens" in California.

ABOUT THE ILLUSTRATOR

A native of the Central Coast of California, Peggy Edwards-Carkeet earned a B.S. in Environmental Studies from the University of California, Berkeley, and, in 1997, a graduate degree in Science Illustration, from the University of California, Santa Cruz.

As a natural science illustrator, and owner of Sierra Nature Prints, Peggy has serviced clients such as Calaveras Big Trees State Park, the Yosemite Association, the Sierra Club, The Nature Conservancy, and the California Department of Fish and Game. Her favorite subjects to illustrate are California native plants and insects, using techniques such as pen and ink, scratchboard, and colored pencil. She is a member of the Guild of Natural Science Illustrators and the California Native Plant Society.

Peggy received numerous awards in the Mother Lode National Art Exhibitions from 1978 to 1984. In 1990, she was awarded first place, Trail Guide Category, from the National Association of Interpretation.

In 1993, Peggy participated in the "Illustrating Nature" show at the Santa Cruz Museum of Natural History, and, in 1994, the "Natural Science Illustration" exhibition at Elkhorn Slough, Moss Landing, California. In 1997, she displayed her artwork in the Oakland Museum of California's "California Species" show.

After an eighteen-year residence near Twain Harte in the Sierra Nevada, Peggy returned to the Central Coast area where she now resides in Scotts Valley next to "an inland marine sandhill habitat".

TABLE OF CONTENTS

WHY ANOTHER WILDFLOWER BOOK?

After residing for almost twenty years in the Midwest, Scottish-born John Muir came to California in 1868. He was one of the first naturalists to extoll the beauty of the magnificent California flora. In his wanderings across this state that first spring and summer, he marvelled at the spectacular flower tapestries he caught sight of everywhere he travelled. Reminiscing years later, he described some vistas of the late 1860s that he had especially enjoyed:

"When California was wild, it was one sweet bee-garden throughout the entire length, north and south, and all the way across from the snowy Sierra to the ocean....The Great Central Plain of California, during the month[s] of March, April, and May, was one smooth, continuous bed of honey-bloom, so marvelously rich that, in walking from one end of it to the other, a distance of four hundred miles, your feet would press more than a hundred flowers at every step."

So it was then—before the land was cleared of trees, shrubs, and "weeds", including wildflowers; so it was then—before much of California's native flora had been irreparably altered or destroyed to make way for agricultural, industrial, or housing development.

Today, it is difficult for us even to imagine wildflowers crowded so closely that for miles no green grass or leaves are visible, so closely that each layer adds its hues to the others as do the tinted layers of a bird's feathers, so closely that at the distant blue horizon, the colors seem to blend to create new colors. Thankfully, in 1998, there are still two large areas in California that give us a hint of the vastness and richness of former displays: Carrizo Plains, in the lower San Joaquin Valley (San Luis Obispo County), and Bear Valley, in the northern Sacramento Valley (Colusa County). Don't fail to visit these areas in the springtime.

Since there is a dearth of information about California native plants available to youth in the public schools, the information in this book is directed to science teachers and their students. It is my hope that even one small fact about each wildflower, lodged in a student's memory, may allow him or her to identify those flowers growing in the wild; and, of course, I want the students to love the wildflowers as I do—wonderful objects of art, each of them.

As educators of elementary school students in environmental education, Peggy and I strongly believe that the conservation and preservation of California's native plants lie in the hands of educated youth. Many environmentalists have focused on saving rare plants one by one, using legal or political means; at times, this has created islands of rare plants which survive in an altered or unnatural habitat. We must teach

1

students to honor *all* plants in an effort to preserve each plant's community.

While there are dozens of wildflower books available to the lay public, there is no one book that includes all of the following: the plant's geographic distribution and its most favored habitat; an accurate description and illustration of the plant, its leaves and its flowers; unique pollinator-flower interrelationships; the origin of the botanical and common names when known; and folklore and historical data when available, including the many uses that native Californians made of indigenous plants. (With few exceptions, the information concerning plant use was gleaned from Barrett and Strike.)

The flowers are presented here, more or less in the order of blooming, from the first blossoms in the valley and lower foothills, then to the upper foothills, and finally to the high mountain meadows. In some instances, one may follow the same flower from the valley floor all the way up to the mountains; for example, the Common Monkeyflower thrives and blooms at all of the elevations.

The wildflowers described are limited to herbaceous plants: plants that are usually soft and green and contain little woody tissue. Most are bulbs, annuals, or perennials; their foliage dies down after the summer droughts or after frosts and then disappears. Many of the plants chosen are flowers that Peggy and I love to share with our students. Others are fairly common and their flowers usually have some unique features that make them more easily recognized.

The scientific names of the wildflowers reflect those appearing in *The Jepson Manual: Higher Plants of California,* as do most of the common names. In the event of a discrepancy in the data from several sources regarding height, width, color, habitat, elevation, or other features, I have used the information in *The Jepson Manual* as the final authority. *The Jepson Manual* had no information concerning times of blooming, so that information was garnered from Munz, *A California Flora.*

In the back of the book, readers will find an Index of the wildflowers by their common and scientific names; the scientific names are shown in italics. Using the Glossary, readers may better understand the botanical terms used repetitiously in the plant descriptions; with the Selected Bibliography, some will be inspired to search out more information.

It is our wish that wildflower enthusiasts, both young and old, will take this book to the meadows, the foothills or mountains—wherever flowers are blooming—and color the drawings, after studying the plants closely. These field-colored illustrations can be taken home for further enjoyment, leaving the wildflowers intact for the next visitor to enjoy.

A NOTE ON THE NAMING OF PLANTS

Every plant belongs to a family and has a family name. Furthermore, each plant has both a Latin first and last name; these Latin names are used throughout the scientific world. The first name, or *genus*, is equivalent to our surname, while the last name, or *species*, corresponds to our given name. Just as there are many people with the same surname, plants also may have several species in a genus. Additionally, some plants have *common names* which are comparable to our nicknames.

Each genus/species has its unique characteristics the whole world over. Common names, on the other hand, can apply to one or several plants. When people want to make sure they are talking about the same plant, they use the genus/species (Latin) names.

For example, *Delphinium patens*, which belongs in the Buttercup Family, is commonly called Spreading Larkspur. In a country foreign to us, and with little knowledge of the language, we probably would not be understood if we inquired whether Spreading Larkspur, a California native plant, grew there—as it is one of over 300 *Delphinium* species worldwide. However, if we asked if they were familiar with *Delphinium patens*, undoubtedly someone could find the answer. Using a botanical description of the plant, a botanist would be able to identify the plant wherever it might be growing.

BUTTERCUPS

In the cold, dark, wet days of January, I seriously doubt that Spring will ever arrive. But, miraculously, Spring always comes. The days always get longer and the wildflowers always bloom. It's time to seek out their beauty and to renew my spirits. By February, I delight in the bright green carpet covering the lower foothills and the Central Valley. Between the intermittent rains, the brilliant blue skies are often spotted with puffs of fluffy white clouds. And, the bright sunshine of the longer days seems almost blinding.

It is then that I race over hill and dale to find the earliest of all spring wildflowers—the Buttercups, *Ranunculus californicus*—dancing on the moist grassy slopes or lolling under the deciduous oaks below 2,000 feet elevation. Later in the year, I relish them in the damp high mountain meadows. It is not surprising that the genus name, *Ranunculus*, Latin for little frog, was chosen since most Buttercups thrive in the wet places where frogs abound.

Buttercups are easily identified by their bright, clear yellow color and their glossy appearance, the latter due to the light reflected off the layer of starch grains located just beneath the yellow pigment cells. They appear as though some fairy or woodland sprite spent hours varnishing and waxing the petals.

Depending upon the species, these perennials are one to two feet tall and freely branching. The leaves, generally wedge-shaped, are divided into threes, then sometimes divided once again. Each leaf may vary from one-half to three inches long.

The flower stems arise from the upper leaf axil—where the leaf joins the stem; the five petal-like sepals are curved downward and lie below the petals. Buttercups, about a half-inch across, usually have seven to nine petals, but some flowers may have over twenty. Additionally, they have large numbers of other flower parts—eighty or so pollen-producing stamens and thirty plus pistils—to collect the pollen from visiting insects. Even though Buttercups have nectar hidden in the back of their flowers, the petals are simple and have no elaborate markings to guide the insects to the nectary.

Native Californian women and children gathered the seeds of Buttercups; afterwards they parched them to remove the husks and the bitter taste. The seeds were then pounded into meal and stored, to be served later as a delicacy for special occasions. To some, this pinole resembled the taste of parched corn; others likened it to popcorn.

4

In the evolutionary plant process, Buttercups are considered to be one of the most "primitive" flowers. Some botanists, early in the 20th century, claimed that all of our flowers descended from this genus. The petals of the ancient flowers were uniform in size and shape; petals were numerous. Often these flowers with multiples of stamens, pistils, and petals had no nectar. Later in the genetic adaptation process, flowers produced nectar to discourage insects from eating the pollen—a smart survival technique.

More "modern" flowers have variously-shaped petals—Lilies, Iris, Bleeding Hearts, and Monkeyflowers, to name a few. With flashy colors and intricate line-patterns indicating the path to the sweet liquid, these more recently-evolved flowers often have only one pistil and three to eight stamens. They usually attract specific pollinators and therefore are more selective than the Buttercups that try, with their excessive proliferation of pollen, to lure any pollinator that's passing by.

Buttercups – *Ranunculus californicus*

When looking for Buttercups, you may notice another plant's spoon-shaped leaves and perhaps a flower or two. Shooting Stars, most often found in full sun, bloom on the heels of the Buttercups. Hurry to find more, as these flowers blush and faint at the slightest hint of summer heat.

SHOOTING STARS

Early in the year, when the temperature first rises and the sun melts away the clouds, Shooting Stars, *Dodecatheon hendersonii,* announce the coming of spring, along with Buttercups. The first blossoms can be found in moist open, grassy areas in the low foothills. They are members of the Primrose Family, as are the cyclamens—common non-native houseplants. Both have skyward-pointing petals, but only Shooting Stars have the exposed, dark, pointed bill.

A striking beauty wherever found, Shooting Stars have several common names: Sailor's Cap, Rooster's Head, Wild Cyclamen, Bird's Bill, and Mosquito Bill. The latter two names may have originated as a result of their pointed stigma tips.

The whorled basal leaves of this perennial emerge several weeks before blooming; each leaf is about the size of a small rounded teaspoon. The leaves are followed by the buds which appear erect on the leafless flower stalk, the scape. At its top, the long flower stalk bears up to thirteen buds arranged like the spokes of a parasol. As the buds open and the flowers grow, the stalk gradually bends and the flowers nod.

The five, sometimes four, petals are rosy-purple with a yellow or white zone at the base of the petal ring. The purple-black anthers and pistil appear to be fused together, forming a "cone", and extend well beyond the petals. The structure of the blossom presents special challenges to its pollinators, especially the large bumblebees that come to dine on the flower's gifts. Since bumblebees cannot hover near the flower as do solitary bees or hummingbirds, they must cling to the fused cone, upside down, while sipping the nectar. They flap their wings vigorously to keep their perch, and in the process shake the pollen onto their bodies.

Shooting Stars, with their swept-back petals, are a sight never to be forgotten. It is no wonder that some of the native Californian women adorned their hair with these beautiful flowers for special ceremonies.

Dodecatheon, from the Greeks, literally means "twelve gods" and some ancients believed these unusual plants were under the protected care of the Deities. There are fourteen species of Shooting Stars, almost all native to North America, of which eight are native to California. Possibly the best known are Henderson's Shooting Stars of the foothills, Jeffrey's Shooting Stars in moist meadows in the ponderosa pine forest up to timberline, and Alpine Shooting Stars found in boggy, high mountain meadows or on wet stream banks above 6000 feet elevation.

Often, the flowers of Shooting Stars are short-lived as the blossoms fade fast with the advent of a short, hot, dry spell. Then the flowers drop, the foliage dries up and this perennial becomes dormant until the following spring, leaving no evidence above ground of its roots resting underneath. If the weather has been too warm, and you didn't find any Shooting Stars in your area, travel up to a higher elevation where the blooming period may be extended into late summer.

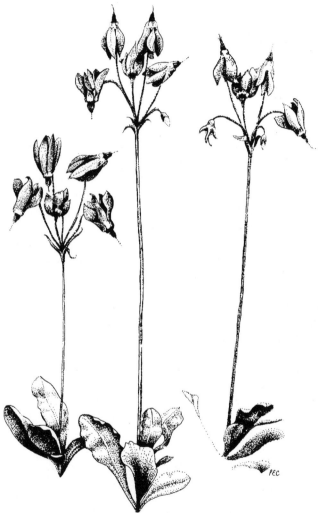

Shooting Stars – *Dodecatheon hendersonii*

After enjoying the Shooting Stars, search the banks and roadsides for the California Poppy, the poppy whose petals sit on a platform. They are everywhere. Then scan the damp fields, meadows, or near creeks for Cream Cups, one of the hairy poppies with drooping buds.

CALIFORNIA POPPY and CREAM CUPS

Perhaps California should be known as the Golden State more for its abundant and diverse flora, favorable climate, fertile soil, and its state flower, the California Poppy, than for the metal sought so diligently by Gold Rush miners in the mid-1800s.

Several centuries ago, when Spanish vessels sailed up and down the newly discovered California coast, the mariners looked inland and observed the hills aflame with orange-colored poppies; they called this the "Land of Fire". So vivid were those carpeted hills in spring, even from far out at sea, that the Spanish mariners of old used the bright colors as beacons.

The California Poppy, *Eschscholzia californica,* is found from Oregon south to Baja California, then east to Arizona and New Mexico. The bluish-green leaves are smooth, finely dissected, fern-like, and arranged alternate on the hairless stems. This poppy has a flat, conspicuous pinkish rim or platform upon which the bud, flower, and later, the seed pod rests. No other poppy has this double rim. The flower, in bud, has a sepal cap that is tightly wrapped around the petals similar to a closed umbrella. This pointed cap falls away as the four petals of the tulip-shaped flower are exposed.

The flowers, two to three inches across, are usually orange, but the color ranges from orange to white. On the same plant, the first blossoms in spring are larger in size and a brighter color than those later in the season. Early Spanish explorers named the California Poppy, *"copa del oro",* meaning cup of gold. They told of a legend in which the orange petals turned to gold, dropped to the ground and then filled the soil with the precious metal. With all the poppies in this state, think what a bonanza that would be for California—if indeed it were true.

In 1817, the Russian ship, Rurik, made port in San Francisco Bay. Aboard were the poet-botanist, Adelbert von Chamisso, and a young doctor from the Baltic, Johann Friedrich Gustav von Eschscholtz. Once ashore, they spied a bright orange flower near the Presidio. Chamisso honored Eschscholtz by naming the California Poppy after him. Somewhere along the way, the "t" was dropped from the genus name. Actually it makes the spelling much easier: E–sch–sch–olzia.

Cream Cups, *Platystemon californicus,* are indeed a member of the Poppy Family, but are in a different genus than the California Poppy. In contrast with California Poppies, the stems and leaves of Cream Cups are coated with delicate hairs. The flower stems rise from a basal cluster of linear leaves which are arranged opposite on the stems. The green-colored buds droop, resembling the buds of a miniature garden poppy. Four to twelve inches tall, Cream Cups have several stems, each with either a bud or a small bowl-shaped flower at its top. They have six petals and numerous stamens. The flowers, less than an inch in diameter, may be variously colored: only white, only yellow, or cream or white with yellow bases. In Greek, *Platystemon* means "broad stamen".

Poppies have no nectar for insect visitors. Instead, the flowers, with their many stamens, produce a plentiful supply of pollen which the bees collect to feed their young. Additionally, small, dark-colored beetles attracted by the flower's spicy fragrance pollinate these plants. They also munch on the petals, leaving small holes in them.

Both California Poppy and Cream Cups are plants of sunshine, opening on bright days and closing each night, or with cloudy skies, to protect the pollen from moisture. The flowers of these poppies are long lasting; each one reopens on several successive days. Because the flowers close in low light or with darkness, the Spanish Californians called them the *"dormidera"*, the drowsy ones.

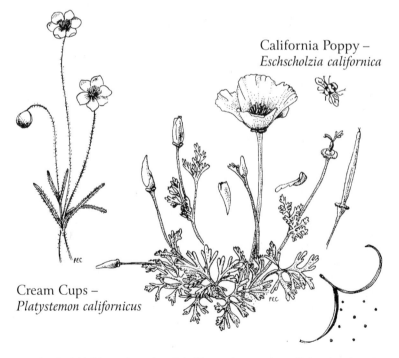

California Poppy –
Eschscholzia californica

Cream Cups –
Platystemon californicus

Leaving behind the poppies, seek out Baby Blue-eyes in grassy places still damp from the spring rains. As with the poppies, stay in the sunshine to locate this flower.

9

BABY BLUE-EYES

In 1819, Thomas Nuttall, a British plant explorer, discovered a new genus of plants in Arkansas. He named the genus *Nemophila,* after the Greek word for woodland- or grove-loving, from the habitat of the plants in the Midwest. However, in California, the *Nemophilas* are most often found in open, moist fields or brushy places rather than in the shade of the woods, and, depending upon the species, are found from 200 to 6000 feet in elevation.

One species, *menziesii,* was named after Archibald Menzies, a Scottish botanist. Also trained in medicine, he served as the surgeon for Captain George Vancouver's expedition to the Americas from 1790 to 1795. They visited California from 1792 to 1794.

An early wildflower, Baby Blue-eyes is often associated with Fivespot, California Poppies, Goldfields, Red Maids, and many other annuals. The leaves of Baby Blue-eyes are one to two inches long and somewhat hairy. Each of the bright green leaves are arranged opposite on the stem and have five to nine rounded lobes.

The buds, and then the inch-wide flowers, pose atop the six- to twelve-inch stems, well above the foliage, so that in a breeze they nod and flutter about in the air like bright blue butterflies.

The five petals of this bowl-shaped flower are azure blue at the rounded tips, white in the center, with dark blue flecks or radiating streaks from the base. To some, those dark lines resemble eyelashes, hence the common name, Baby Blue-eyes. The petals of other Baby Blue-eyes may be very light blue, some almost white. The flowers open and close in response to the air temperature, the petals folding inward at night or in the cold. Extreme heat shortens the blooming period.

Generally, in the hills, fields or meadows, these plants cling so closely to the ground that their leaves become inconspicuous as they are swallowed up by the growing grasses and other herbs. Then suddenly on some warm sunny day, they arise as if crowds of them decided to burst open simultaneously, much as music bursts forth in unison from the orchestra at the command of the conductor's baton. In some parts of California, these crowds of Baby Blue-eyes appear as brilliant bright blue pools visible from great distances. It is a wondrous sight to behold.

Another member of this genus, *N. heterophylla,* the Small-flowered Nemophila or Baby White-eyes, hovers at the edge of the woods, or on grassy slopes interfacing the brush, seeking out a finite amount of sunlight. The white, half-inch flowers stand high above the leaves, appearing as a white miniature version of Baby Blue-eyes. This species also blooms in profusion, lighting up the woods with a frothy whiteness above the bright green grass of early spring.

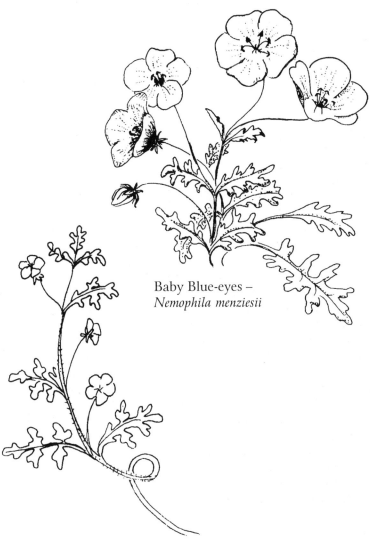

Baby Blue-eyes –
Nemophila menziesii

Baby White-eyes – *Nemophila heterophylla*

About the same time that Baby Blue-eyes are blossoming, you might chance upon some bulb-like plants with white or purple flowers on stems one to two feet tall. Swaying in the breeze, the flowers of White and Blue Brodiaea are held in a cluster, high above the strap-like or linear leaves.

11

BLUE BRODIAEA and WHITE BRODIAEA

The beautiful cluster lilies with genus names such as *Brodiaea,* *Dichelostemma,* and *Triteleia* are all commonly called Brodiaeas. In the early part of this century, they were called cluster lilies because of the compact head of flowers. All are members of the Lily Family whose flower parts—petals, sepals, stamens—occur in threes or multiples of three.

Brodiaeas are indigenous to western North America, native nowhere else in the world. However, in their growing range from the valley floor to the mountain meadows, they are abundant and represented by various species. Even in the harsh climate of the serpentine foothills areas, you might find eight or nine different species if you made repeated visits from March through June, Wild Hyacinth, Ithuriel's Spear, Pretty Face, and Harvest Brodiaea, to name a few. But, without fail, if you visit in March and April, you will see the Blue Brodiaea, sometimes called Blue Dicks, and the White Brodiaea or White Hyacinth.

Blue Brodiaea, *Dichelostemma capitatum,* is the most common of all and is the earliest of any to appear. In California west of the Sierra Nevada, Blue Brodiaea is usually found on coastal hills and plains and in the foothills below the ponderosa pine forest. The four to ten blue-violet flowers are contained in a tight head atop a leafless two- to three-foot stalk. The grasslike leaves, six to ten inches long, have often dried up and vanished by the time the flowers blossom.

The bulbs of Blue Brodiaea were one of the most important underground food plants of the Sierra Miwoks. They were harvested with hardwood digging sticks made from the native mountain mahogany. When the native Californians were gathering the bulbs, they took extreme care to ensure that the flowers were attached so as to avoid harvesting the deadly Death Camas which sometimes grows in the same area but has white flowers.

Arranged at the top of the flower stalk like the spokes of a wheel, the head of star-like flowers of White Brodiaea, *Triteleia hyacinthina,* may contain as many as fifty individual flowers. Each petal has a central line of green on the outside which is faintly green inside the flower. Some petals may have deep lavender veinings instead of green if the plants have been standing in water.

To find the White Brodiaea, look at the edges of intermittent creeks or along stream banks from the valley floor to the upper foothills. Sometimes in August, the plants at higher elevations are so prolific that the masses of blossoms whiten the damp mountain meadows as they wave in the breezes.

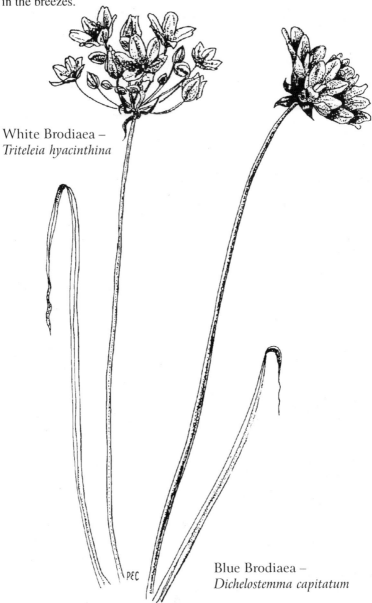

White Brodiaea –
Triteleia hyacinthina

Blue Brodiaea –
Dichelostemma capitatum

While you were studying the Blue Brodiaea, you may have spotted, nearby, a light purple flower with a dark eye. Or you might have seen a plant with a blue-purple head of flowers, happily growing in the roadside ditch. For more treats, check out the Gilias soon.

13

BIRD'S EYES and GLOBE GILIA

Bird's Eyes, *Gilia tricolor,* grow on open grasslands, hills, and valleys from the California coast, through the Central Valley, then up to about 3600 feet elevation in the Sierra foothills. From a distance, this delicate and airy plant paints the landscape with a light lavender color when blooming.

An upright annual about twelve inches high, this flower has many side branches extending from the main stem. The light green leaves at the base of the plant are twice divided and held in loose clusters. Further up the stem, narrow, linear leaves are numerous in the axils—the area where the side branches join the main stem.

The flowers, two to three per stem, sit on the uppermost branches. Five petals join at their bases to form a short trumpet. The upper parts of the petals are pale to deep blue-violet, often fading to a lighter color inside. At the top of the trumpet's throat, five pairs of dark purple dots or marks encircle the entrance to the bright yellow nectar tube. Completing this visual feast, the stamens extend up well beyond the petals, showing off their rich blue anthers—a color similar to that of the bluebird.

According to some, the deep yellow centers below the dark purple ring reminded nature lovers of the varicolored eyes of certain birds, suggesting the common name, Bird's Eyes. The species name, *tricolor,* undoubtedly originated from the fact that one can see three distinct colors in the flowers.

Another *Gilia* species, *capitata ssp. capitata,* often seen on the gravelly roadsides in the foothills, cannot be mistaken for any other plant with its blue puffballs and delicate foliage. Globe Gilia is found from British Columbia to Baja California, growing in fields, on banks or disturbed areas, in chaparral or oak woodlands, up to 6000 feet elevation. Unlike Bird's Eyes, each Globe Gilia plant has only one unbranched flower stem which sometimes reaches three feet, though more commonly it is only a foot high. Like other *Gilia* species, Globe Gilia is also characterized by its deeply-cut compound leaves that are arranged alternate on the stem. The basal leaves, up to four inches long, are slashed into fine segments. The stem's upper leaves are much smaller and even more lacy than the lower leaves.

Though more often powder-blue, the dense, round, one-and-one-half-inch flower heads may range in color from light to deep blue, to blue-purple, or sometimes even white. While Bird's Eyes have only two or three flowers per stem, Globe Gilia may have fifty to one hundred tiny

14

flowers crowded into one dense cluster. The stamens of each small flower are longer than the petals so that the head appears to have numerous pins in its cushion. From a distance, the flower ball has a fuzzy appearance. *Capitata* refers to the rounded head of clustered flowers, hence the common name, Globe Gilia. *Gilia*, pronounced "Hee–lee–a", is named after Gil, an early Spanish botanist.

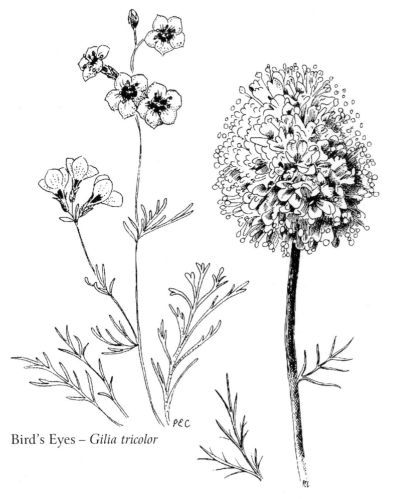

Bird's Eyes – *Gilia tricolor*

Globe Gilia – *Gilia capitata* ssp. *capitata*

In the shade of oaks and pines, glance at the dense lacy foliage of the Bleeding Hearts, busy modeling their pink dressy blossoms shoulders above the leaves. Later in the year, at the edge of the snowbanks, observe Steer's Head—a tiny one-leafed plant with a pale pink skull-like flower.

BLEEDING HEARTS and STEER'S HEAD

Both Bleeding Hearts and Steer's Head, members of the Poppy Family, have flowers with most unusual shapes. After your first careful observation of the "hearts" and "skulls", you won't need a botanist or even the botanists' bible, *The Jepson Manual,* to ever identify them again.

From central California to British Columbia, Bleeding Hearts, *Dicentra formosa,* thrive in damp, partially-shaded places in oak woodlands and coniferous forests up to 7000 feet elevation. However, more profuse displays may be seen in the Sierran meadows where the nodding blossoms snuggle closely together, just clearing the green herbage.

Bleeding Hearts, a perennial with fleshy horizontally-growing rootstalks, stands eight to eighteen inches tall. The finely-dissected leaves, arranged on a long stalk, are lacy, fernlike, and blue-green in color.

The rosy-purple blossoms in small, branched clusters are borne on stalks separate from the leaves. Though the sides of the two outer petals are fused together to form a pouch in the shape of a heart, the tip of the three-fourths-inch flower is open. There are two slots at that tip, each one holding three united stamens. The other two petals, inside the heart, form the dangling spurs which beckon the pollinators with their dark reddish color. It matters not from which side the insects savor the honey, as the pollen can be taken from inside either opening to pollinate the next heart they visit.

One day I discovered that pollinator. A large bumblebee flew to a flower and, suspended upside down like a rock climber negotiating an overhang, clasped the heart with its two front legs. Each time the bee landed on a blossom, the flower stalk, bent down from the bee's weight, bobbed up and down like the wooden horses on the merry-go-round. After drinking its fill of nectar, the bumblebee released its hold and the stalk sprang back to an upright position—temporarily—until the bee latched on to an adjacent flower for more nectar.

Steer's Head, *Dicentra uniflora,* though considered by many to be a rare plant, is more rarely seen than it is rare. Like Bleeding Hearts, it, too, is a perennial. Growing at elevations from 6000 to 12000 feet in fine gravel or on rocky slopes, the stems of the leaf and flower spring up, separately, from the ground just after the snow melts. The key to locating this plant is to know what the leaf looks like. It is small, up to two inches long, gray-green, and dissected into many small lobes. Usually lying flat on the ground, the leaves most often are asymmetrical. Steer's Head

16

commonly has only one leaf though some plants may have as many as three.

This tiny plant has a total height of one to four inches when blossoming, and bears only one flower which is about a half-inch wide and pinkish-white in color. The four petals and two sepals jointly form the shape of a steer's head. The flower conjures up a vision from the desert, but in miniature: a sun-bleached steer's skull with its long, bony snout, hollow eye sockets, and upturned horns.

Once you recognize its leaves, know where it grows, and can predict when the snow will melt on the high mountain slopes, you will easily find it in the same place year after year. After all, it's a tuber and it won't be moving very far.

The genus name, *Dicentra,* means "twice spurred", referring to the two spurs at the heart's point; *formosa* (Bleeding Hearts) denotes a beautiful flower, and *uniflora* (Steer's Head), very simply, means "one flower".

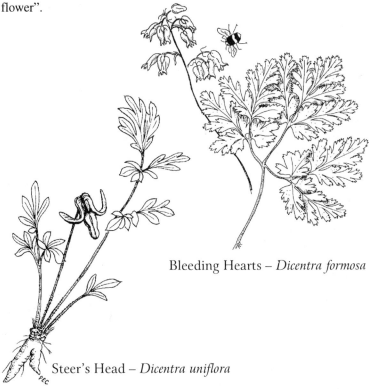

Bleeding Hearts – *Dicentra formosa*

Steer's Head – *Dicentra uniflora*

From the shaded haunts of Bleeding Hearts, look past the hills to sunny, open places. Sometimes you'll see blankets of yellow aster-type flowers displaying their dazzling jewelry. And, if you walk through a thick patch of the Goldfields, your shoes will take on a brilliant hue.

GOLDFIELDS

The Gold Rush prospectors in the foothills or the valley didn't have to look very far in the spring to find gold. This small annual, Goldfields, filled vast stretches of lowlands and hills, either coastal or inland, with a blanket of brilliant yellow.

Lasthenia californica, a member of the Aster Family, is one of the earliest wildflowers to bloom in the spring. Ubiquitous in California, this four- to eight-inch plant is found on sun-drenched areas, up to 4500 feet elevation; not endemic to California, it also grows in southwest Oregon, the western Mojave Desert, and central Arizona, as well as northern Baja California.

As noted in Jepson's *A Manual of the Flowering Plants of California,* 1925, the genus name *Lasthenia,* "remembers a Greek girl who, in order to attend the lectures of Plato, dressed in the garb of a man".

Members of the Aster Family are also known as "composites" as each flower head often contains two sets of flowers: the disk florets compacted in the middle, and petal-like ray florets extending out clockwise from the center. Familiar wildflowers in this family include Tidy-tips, Mules Ears, Pearly Everlasting, and, of course, Dandelions, Asters, and Daisies.

Using your hand lens, look closely at the disk and ray florets; you may be able to see the stamens and pistils. If not, carefully remove a ray "petal" and notice its flower parts; the disk florets are so small that you may need a pair of tweezers to hold them while you make your scientific observations.

You can identify this charming plant by its yellow flower head, one-half to one inch in diameter, with ten to fourteen ray flowers, reaching out in wheel-like fashion from the slightly-darkened disk flowers. The flower head is wrapped underneath with a rosette of leaf-like green parts called bracts. The plant's greenish leaves, needlelike and up to one inch in length, are arranged opposite on the reddish-colored stems. The stems and leaves, as well as the underneath parts of the flower, are sparsely covered with sharp, stiff hairs.

In its natural habitat, Goldfields is pollinated by small solitary bees who live singly in underground areas near the blooming flowers. By blossom time, the bees have carved out underground cells where they will store the flower pollen to provide food for their developing larvae. These "bees" actually resemble small flies more than bees—hence another common name, Fly Flower.

Goldfields was important to several tribes of native Californians. They gathered seeds of these plants in early summer, then parched and crushed them into a flour. This was eaten dry or as a mush after mixing with water.

If you've ever had the good fortune to be in the Carrizo Plains, west of Bakersfield, in late March or early April, you know that your shoes become golden from the pollen as you walk through the thickly-clothed patches of Goldfields.

Goldfields – *Lasthenia californica*

Now leave the sunny spots and trudge over to rest near the cool dampness of the north-facing slopes. From a distance, you'll catch sight of horizontal lines of white and purple. Drawing nearer, behold the Chinese Houses with their flaring roof tiles.

CHINESE HOUSES and TINCTURE PLANT

Chinese Houses and Tincture Plant, both of the genus, *Collinsia,* are in the *Scrophulariaceae* or Figwort Family. Affectionately called "Scrophs" (rhymes with "coughs"), this family includes many gorgeous wildflowers such as Purple Owl's Clover, Penstemon, Indian Warrior, Elephant's Head, Indian Paintbrush, Butter-and-Eggs, and Monkeyflower. Each of these cousins has five, irregularly-shaped petals that are painted with one or more colors of the rainbow.

Blooming from March to June, Chinese Houses, *Collinsia heterophylla,* are found up to 3000 feet elevation—often on cooler, north-facing slopes in oak woodlands or openings in the chaparral. *Heterophylla,* the species name, means that the leaves are different on the stems of the same plant. The genus was named in honor of Zachaeus Collins, an American botanist in the early 1800s.

An annual growing to a foot or more in height, Chinese Houses usually prefer moist and shady places, though they may be found in some sunny spots, provided their feet are kept damp enough. In the sun, they appear more vigorous and their stems are often branched, unlike the stems of those in the shade. The lower leaves on the stems are broadly oblong, up to two-and-one-half inches long, with barely visible, toothed margins; sometimes the outer edges of the bright green leaves are faintly scalloped. The long, egg-shaped upper leaves clasp the stem just below the first row of blossoms. Velvety fuzz often covers the entire plant, including the flowers.

The petals, less than an inch long, are joined partway to form a tube. The throat of the flower opens into two parts: the upper lip has two erect white petals, each with dark purple dots in the center and a dark violet line at its base; the three flaring petals of the lower part are violet to rose-purple. The middle lobe of the bottom lip, generally with a very dark red tip, is folded into a keel-shaped pouch which encloses the four stamens, style, and nectar-producing glands. While the many tiers of blossoms rising on the slender stems suggest the different levels of a Chinese pagoda, the lower petals, gradually curving outward, mimic the shape of the pagoda's flaring roof tiles.

Chinese Houses were discovered in the 1820s by David Douglas, who collected them for European gardens. Seeds of many California native plants that were horticulturally successful in Europe were brought back to this country. Such was the case with Chinese Houses. According to Parsons, in the early 1900s, it was popular in the eastern United States and was called Innocence.

You might walk past Tincture Plant, *Collinsia tinctoria,* unless you pay heed to every blossoming flower you see, as its blue-greyish-white petals don't leap out at you. However, its flowers might attract your attention at they are arranged in tiers or rows, similar to Chinese Houses.

While Chinese Houses bloom in mid-spring, Tincture Plant blooms from June to August. It is found in rocky, dry woodlands or coniferous forests from 1800 to 7500 feet in elevation. Sometimes, this six- to twenty-four-inch plant grows in such abundance, and so closely together, that it appears to be an underground creeper, rather than an annual.

The leaves of Tincture Plant are sticky, and as the species name suggests, will stain the fingers and hands a brown color similar to that from tincture of iodine. The oval leaves are arranged opposite each other on the stems and the edges of the leaves are often mottled.

All five petals, one-half to three-fourths inch long, are white and delicately decorated. While the upper two petals have a yellowish base with blue speckles, the lower three petals are distinctly veined with dark purple. Close up, in its own quiet, retiring way, Tincture Plant is every bit as beautiful as the more colorful Chinese Houses.

Chinese Houses –
Collinsia heterophylla

PEC

Investigate the glistening yellow flowers bordering creeks and intermittent waterways or pools. The saucy red-dotted faces of Monkeyflowers beckon you to come closer.

21

COMMON MONKEYFLOWER

Common Monkeyflower, *Mimulus guttatus,* is distributed over most of California from the valley floor up to 7500 feet elevation in the mountains. It is also found as far north as Alaska, east in the Rockies, and south in Mexico. Its favorite haunts are in damp or wet places near springs or seeps and at streamside. Sometimes, you might even find the flowers and leaves floating in pools of water, though its feet are firmly planted in the earth.

A perennial, this Monkeyflower varies in height from two to three feet in the foothills to only about three inches tall in the high mountains. From plant to plant, the size and shape of the leaves are determined both by the water supply and the composition of the soil. Under optimal conditions, the smooth, bright green leaves are roundish to oval-shaped, about one-half to three inches long and unevenly toothed. They are arranged opposite each other, sometimes clasping the stem, other times on a petiole—the leaf stalk. Likewise, the size of the flowers, from one-third to one inch across, seems to vary more with the amount of moisture available than from the effects of altitude, soil, or adverse weather conditions.

Most *Mimulus* species have five irregularly-shaped petals which form a two-lipped ring of petals—the corolla. The two petals of the upper lip are turned back, the lower three are turned down. Different from many Monkeyflowers, the throat of *M. guttatus* is nearly closed; the center lower petal with its hairy palate almost touches the upper petals. Furthermore, the petals of the lower lip are longer and wider than those of the lip above. This provides an excellent landing pad for small flying insects that are attracted to the flower by the bright red, freckle-like faces on the canary-yellow petals. The weight of the insect on the lower lip causes it to drop down like a trap door, bringing into view the end of the red-dotted trail at the nectary.

The two-part, club-shaped lips of the stigma, the pollen-receiving part of the flower, extend upward into and above the flower's throat. The stigma of a fresh flower will close after being touched lightly with a straw or the fingertips. But, you can't fool the flower. Minutes later, the lips re-open, poised for an insect's load of pollen. After the pollen is delivered, the stigma immediately clamps shut and remains closed. The process of seed-making begins.

In times long past, the leaves and tender young stalks were eaten as greens by native Californians and early settlers. Sometimes, the native

Californians burned the leaves and used the ashes as a source of salt.

Mimulus means "mimic" or "mime"; *guttatus,* from the Latin, means "droplike spot" or "speckled". With a bit of imagination, the flowers can remind one of an impish monkey as its common name implies: the upper petals suggest the ears and forehead of the monkey; the lower petals, suggest the puffy cheeks, and nose and mouth.

Common Monkeyflower
– *Mimulus guttatus*

PEC

Reluctantly, the time has come to leave this speckle-faced little monkey behind to meet up with Fivespot, a cousin of Baby Blue-eyes, accompanied by satiny Red Maids.

FIVESPOT and RED MAIDS

Fivespot and Red Maids are lumped together, not because of botanic kinship, but by their habitat association. In early spring in the serpentine soils of the foothills, you will often find Fivespot and Red Maids side by side on moist, sunny, grassy slopes. The spreading succulent stems of Red Maids weave over, under, and between the leaves of Fivespot—so much so that it's difficult to separate out each plant amidst the small red and large white flowers.

Fivespot, *Nemophila maculata,* is native to the Sierra foothills and mountain slopes below 7500 feet from Nevada County in the north to Kern County in the south. (It has a much more limited range than its cousin, Baby Blue-eyes.) A low growing plant up to twelve inches tall, it is not conspicuous since it blends with other herbs until the mass of white buds bursts open, seemingly all at once. The leaves of Fivespot are rounded with five to seven deep lobes, somewhat hairy, and arranged opposite on the stems.

Fivespot was so named because of the dark blue-purple spot at the tip of each of the five petals. The white flowers are large, up to two inches in diameter. *Nemophila* means "lover of the grove"—a moist partially-shaded place. The species name, *maculata,* means "spotted" or "blotched", suggesting other common names: Calico Flower and Spotted Nemophila.

Fivespot was introduced into cultivation in England in 1848, and this brings to mind an interesting story. Theodor Hartweg, a German botanist, spent nearly seven years in Central and South America collecting plants and seeds for the Royal Horticultural Society of England. After completing a season of collecting on his second expedition to the Americas, he sought transportation from Mexico to California. In 1846, after refusals from several countries, including the United States, Hartweg gained passage to Monterey, California on a British ship. A month after his arrival in Monterey, on July 7, the American flag was hoisted and hostilities between Mexico and the United States began. Despite the conflict, he wanted to botanize in California and therefore needed animals to take him to remote areas. Unfortunately, all available horses had been seized by the Mexican commandant, Jose Castro, who viewed all strangers with suspicion. Though Hartweg finally found equine transportation, Castro remained dubious of Hartweg's motives and found it unbelievable "that a person would come all the way from London to look after the weeds." Fivespot was one of the "weeds" that Hartweg collected.

A low-growing annual from two to twelve inches high, Red Maids,

Calandrinia ciliata, is found in open places with grasses or other herbage, from Vancouver, British Columbia down to lower California at elevations below 6000 feet. The stems branch from the base of the plant, sometimes erect, though more often trailing on the ground. The fleshy, linear leaves, one to three inches long, appear alternately on the stems.

The bowl-shaped, satiny flowers are arranged at the end of the stem, singly or in loose spikes. Each of the five magenta-colored petals is veined with a slightly darker red color. Further down the petals, the color of the flower's throat fades to near white. In sharp contrast with Fivespot, the flowers of Red Maids are much smaller, often no more than three-fourths inch wide. The blossoms have a delicate, somewhat musky perfume; each flower lasts but one day, opening only with bright sunshine.

The genus name, *Calandrinia,* was given in honor of J. L. Calandrini, a Swiss mathematics and philosophy professor who wrote a botany book in the early 18th century. The species name, *ciliata,* refers to the few fringes on the edges of the petals.

Red Maids, in times past, were a source of human food. Native Californians ate the fleshy leaves and stems, either raw or cooked. The slender taproots were an important staple in the Miwok diet. They also gathered the dark seeds, parched them with coals, then pulverized and pressed them into cakes for eating. Other tribes harvested the petals which were mixed with the seeds and then rolled into balls; they relished this confection much as we do ⬚ candy. Coast Miwoks crushed flowers and rubbed the paste ⬚ on their faces for coloring.

Fivespot – *Nemophila maculata* and Red Maids – *Calandrinia ciliata*

While stretching in the sunshine, let's wander past the bright silky Red Maids and the purple-blotched Fivespot to stand amidst a sea of Butter-and-Eggs. From a distance, they have an uneven texture like that of lumpy scrambled eggs.

BUTTER-and-EGGS

In early spring, solid carpets of yellow are common in the landscape of the foothills, grasslands, valleys, and coastal areas. There seems to be a continuous display of gold for several weeks as various genera of plants burst forth with bloom, but you'll see different shades of yellow and varying plant heights and shapes as the season moves along.

When the bright blankets of Goldfields are beginning to fade, an expanse of yet another yellow flower, Butter-and-Eggs, appears on the scene. Johnny-tucks, as they are also known, are lighter in color and not quite so brilliant as Goldfields since the white in the throat of the flower seems to dilute it a bit. Also, the purplish leaves, stems and bracts, and the flower's purple hooked beak create dark holes in the golden floral carpet. From a distance, the fields of *Triphysaria eriantha* have a lumpy appearance, like that of scrambled eggs, and not like the smooth, flat-topped color most often seen in the acres of Goldfields.

Growing up to a foot high, Butter-and-Eggs is found throughout California and northward to southwest Oregon. The leaves on the branching stems are one-half to two inches long, arranged alternate on the stem and divided into several thread-like parts.

Blooming from March to May, the half-inch flowers are clustered near the tips of the slender stem. Look closely: you'll see five petals extending out of the fused-petal throat. The floral tube has a distinct right-angled jog at its top. Each of the three bright yellow lower petals, puffed up like tiny balloons, have two greenish-yellow spots. The upper two petals form a point, dark purple in color, which extends above and beyond the lower petals.

Bees and other flying insects alight on the lower petals and weigh them down. This causes the petals to open and exposes the shallow nectary. The stamens, enclosed in the purple beak, dust pollen on the insect's back as it moves in and out of the flower to savor the sweet liquid. Butter-and-Eggs have an oblong fruit which contains thirty to fifty dark brown tiny seeds.

The origin of the genus name, *Triphysaria,* is from the Greeks and means "three bladders," referring to the inflated pouches of the three lower petals. Recent research has indicated that all members of this genus are hemiparasites. These are plants that can live and prosper on their own, but, when given the chance, will hook into the aqueous-nutrient system of various grasses, ceanothus, sagebrush, and many other unsuspecting host plants. Fortunately for both, the "invading" plants do not kill their providers as they partake of the water and minerals collected from the soil and air, or the sugars manufactured by the host. If these hemiparasites were people, we would call them "free-loaders".

Butter-and-Eggs – *Triphysaria eriantha*

In early spring, track down a plant with large leaves like a dog's tongue, growing at the edge of the woods or chaparral. Drawing near to this flower, study the pale blue blossoms of Hound's Tongue with their pearly-white beads and wheel-like faces.

HOUND'S TONGUE

One of many spring-blooming wildflowers, Hound's Tongue, *Cynoglossum grande,* grows profusely in cool, moist places, stretching out into open areas or sunny meadows of the oak woodlands or coniferous forests. In chaparral country, maybe only a solitary plant will peek out from under the shrubby skirt of a manzanita or ceanothus as if hiding away, relishing the shade in the dry country.

The genus name, *Cynoglossum,* is derived from two Greek words meaning "dog" and "tongue". To some, the size and texture of the large leaves resemble the tongues of dogs. The species name, *grande,* extolls the majesty of this regal plant.

A perennial, you'll find Hound's Tongue from central California to as far north as British Columbia. The three- to six-inch-long stems, bearing leaves of a similar length, emerge in a circle from the base of the plant. Where attached to the stem, the base of the leaf is heart-shaped or rounded while the tip of the leaf is usually pointed. The under surfaces of the one- to four-inch-wide leaves are covered with many fine hairs, but the upper sides are smooth.

The seven to nine flower heads, in a coil like the neck of a fiddle, sit near the top of the smooth stalks, rising about eighteen inches above the leaves. Opening one by one down the flower stalk, each coil with four to six pinkish-colored buds gradually unwinds. The blossoms have a pretty, wheel-like face: five clear, bright blue petals extend from the shortened trumpet throat. A ring or collar of white surrounds the throat at its base, appearing as tiny, pearly-white beads, two per petal.

The fruit of the Hound's Tongue—four hard, brown, almost spherical seeds—is approximately one-fourth inch long. The upper surfaces of the seeds are covered with short barbed prickles that easily attach to clothing or animal fur. As a result, the seeds remain on the fur or clothing until picked off, one by one. Several genera in this family are aptly named Stickseed.

Considerable folklore surrounds this plant. One author noted that in medieval times, some believed that if you laid the leaves under your feet, dogs wouldn't bark at you because the leaves "tied the tongues of dogs". Additionally, Dioscorides, a Greek physician, stated that "the leaves, beaten small, with old swine grease hath the power to heal things bitten of dogs". Heeding such advice today might lead to an unnecessary and painful death. But in those times, if the animal was rabid, there was no possibility of a cure, so people kept searching and experimenting.

Though few native Californians used Hound's Tongue for food, several tribes cooked the roots and ate them for medicinal purposes—to relieve colic or stomach ulcers. Also, poultices of the roots were used to alleviate pain and swelling from scalds and burns as well as for general inflammation.

At a distance, this shy plant does not attract much attention from passersby because of its dull bluish-green leaves and light blue flowers, especially when seen in the bright, blinding sunlight of midday. However, its delicate flowers reward the wildflower enthusiasts who leave their cars behind and traipse through the woods to find them.

Hound's Tongue – *Cynoglossum grande*

Gaze past the shaded woods of Hound's Tongue into the open fields, seemingly covered with a white dust. Then stroll over to examine the Popcorn Flowers decorated with white-beaded throats like those of its close relative, Hound's Tongue.

29

POPCORN FLOWER

Blooming from March to May, these forget-me-not-like flowers are most welcome, filling the air with their subtle fragrance. Tiny white blossoms cluster together at the tip of the stem to give the appearance of a popped kernel of corn.

Singly, each head of "popped" corn is not very showy. However, with an abundance of plants, and with each Popcorn Flower seemingly trying to stretch just a bit higher than its neighbor in the grassy fields, a white quilt covers the landscape, similar to the color and texture of a light snowfall. The native Californian children called the flowers Snowdrops; the Spanish Californians named them "nievitas", meaning "little snow".

Plagiobothrys, the genus name, is derived from two Greek words: "plagio", meaning on the side, and "bothrus", a pit or excavation—an allusion to the scooped out sides of each seed. When this genus was named, it was the first known fruit having a hollow scar.

The six- to eighteen-inch stems of this slender annual plant branch from the base. The more vigorous of the two branches splits again at a slightly higher level, creating the appearance of a three-pronged stem. The stems and leaves are bristly, with coarse or shaggy hairs which give them a whitish cast. Most of the leaves are basal, in a rosette, and about one to four inches long. The flower stalk is scantily clad with tiny leaves. Juice from the roots, stems, and mid-rib of the leaves stains the fingers a reddish-purple. The roots of some species contain a rich purple dye.

The flowers are arranged in a coil at the top of the stem. The five short petals, each one-fourth to one-third inch across, join together at their base, creating the funnel-shaped flower. A telltale ring of forget-me-not-like white beads almost obscures the opening of the flower's throat.

Popcorn Flowers are separated into species by the characteristics of their fruits, which usually consists of three, but sometimes four, seedlike nutlets. Identification of each of the species is most difficult.

The common foothill species, *nothofulvus,* blooms in fields or on hillsides, mostly below 2500 feet elevation. There are other foothill species, as well as a mountain Popcorn Flower growing from 4000 to 11000 feet elevation.

Native Californians used this plant in many ways. Described as sweet and aromatic, the crisp, tender shoots and flowers furnished springtime food. Later in the year, the seeds were gathered in large quantities to make pinole. Women and children used the dye obtained from the base of the young leaves to stain their cheeks crimson.

How can one tell whether the white flowers in the fields are Popcorn Flowers, or other white-blossoming plants? Viewing from a distance, if the flowers rise above the grassy slopes and wave in the breeze, they undoubtedly are Popcorn Flowers. Hike over to see if you guessed right.

Popcorn Flower – *Plagiobothrys nothofulvus*

Earlier, you may have noticed grasslike leaves, one to two feet high, while hunting for wildflowers on the sunny slopes. Now, saunter over to the yellow, pink, or white flowers and peek into the petal bowls of Pussy Ears, Fairy Lanterns, and Mariposas to admire the intricate patterns of some *Calochortus* species.

PUSSY EARS, FAIRY LANTERNS, and MARIPOSA LILIES

There are about sixty species of the genus *Calochortus* that are native to western North America—from the Dakotas westward to British Columbia and then south to Guatemala. In California alone, there are at least thirty-seven species of this bulb.

In this state, you'll find them in sunny places—in grasslands or forest clearings—from the sandy soils of the hot foothills to the gravelly slopes of the high mountains. Dependent upon the species and the elevation, the leaves—thin and grasslike—normally die down before the plant blooms from April to August.

The genus name, *Calochortus,* is derived from two Greek words: "kallos" meaning beautiful and "chortos" for grass. Beautiful Grass is another of its common names. While all *Calochortus* species have three petals, three sepals, and six stamens, the general shape of the blossoms varies considerably between species. They can be described either as a shallow bowl, a globe, or a deep-cupped tulip.

Star Tulips have small flowers about one-half inch across, arranged in the shape of a shallow bowl. One of the Star Tulips, Pussy Ears *(Calochortus monophyllus),* is so named because the petals are adorned with colorful hairs which are soft to the touch like a kitten's ear. This plant usually has only one strap-like leaf, hence the species name, *monophyllus.* You'll find these three- to four-inch-high plants in openings of the pine forest with colors of pink, purple, yellow, or white.

The Fairy Lanterns or Globe Tulips have nodding flowers whose petals overlap to form a closed globe. They give the impression of shyness, just barely looking out from the edge of the woods using their lanterns to show the way. They may be all white or various soft shades of pink, purple, or yellow on stems usually eight to twelve inches tall, but sometimes reaching over two feet. *Calochortus albus,* as the species name tells us, is a white Fairy Lantern.

The Mariposas, with deep-cup or tulip-shaped flowers about two inches across, display beautiful artwork inside the flower near the nectary at the base of the petals. The nectar gland of each species has its own unique shape and is often covered with hairs in various patterns and colors.

The Mariposas have the greatest variations, both in petal markings and colors, and, of all of the Mariposas, the White Mariposa Lily, *Calochortus venustus,* shows the greatest differences from flower to flower; they can be white, light cream, pale yellow, pink, purple, or even deep maroon-red in color on stems up to two feet tall. There may be only a few lines or splotches on some, while others display a riot of colorful designs. Perhaps the latter was the reason the Spanish chose their word, "mariposa", meaning "butterfly", to describe this flower whose petals are reminiscent of butterfly wings.

Native Californians harvested Mariposa bulbs in late spring. As the bulbs kept only four or five days before shriveling, they couldn't be stored for future use; so the bulbs were eaten raw, cooked, or ground into meal. The California natives thought that the Mariposas were a special gift because they yielded life-giving food from dry barren slopes. They honored it by calling it Life Plant.

Mariposa Lily –
Calochortus venustus

Fairy Lantern –
Calochortus albus

Pussy Ears – *Calochortus monophyllus*

Growing in the same sunny locale with *Calochortus* are other handsome flowers: the wispy, soft, gauzy blue-violet of Ithuriel's Spear and the clear pink of Snake Lily and the reddish-purple, satiny sheen of Harvest Brodiaea together with the saucy, bright yellow stars of Pretty Face. Each of these close relatives pulls us in various directions demanding our immediate attention, like a roomful of preschoolers.

ITHURIEL'S SPEAR, TWINING BRODIAEA, HARVEST BRODIAEA, and PRETTY FACE

These four Brodiaeas are closely related to the White Brodiaea and Blue Brodiaea that we discovered earlier. As the weather continues to warm up, you'll find all of them in the ponderosa pine forest up to about 4500 feet elevation. Above that altitude, we leave Ithuriel's Spear *(Triteleia laxa)* and Twining Brodiaea *(Dichelostemma volubile)* behind, but Harvest Brodiaea *(Brodiaea elegans)* continues to grow up to 7000 feet; the mountain maid, Pretty Face *(Triteleia ixioides)* hikes up even higher to 9000 feet in or near the montane coniferous forests.

Ithuriel's Spear usually has light violet or blue-purple flowers, eight to forty-eight in number, in an open umbel. (The short stems of the tiny flowers branch out from the main flower stem in an umbrella-like or spoke-like fashion.) Only rarely will you find white or light pink ones. Compared with Blue Brodiaea, these tubular flowers are larger, about three-fourths inch long, and in a looser cluster, not a tight head as that of Blue Brodiaea. In Milton's *Paradise Lost,* Ithuriel was one of the cherubim sent by Gabriel to search for Satan. Touched by Ithuriel's spear, Satan was revealed. Some plant-lover of long ago likened the straight slimness of the tall flower stem of *T. laxa* to the spear borne by Ithuriel.

Depending on the amount of moisture and the richness of the soil, the flower stems of *T. laxa* can be but a few inches tall to about four feet. Growing on clay soils in fields, open grasslands, or brush, it seems as if the main stem reaches just high enough for the flowers to see above the grasses as they sway in the breeze.

It's quite a shock to look into the shrubby brush and see what appears to be a bright pink, translucent snake about the size of a pencil. Further investigation, however, gives relief. Blooming after Ithuriel's Spear, the snake-like Twining Brodiaea (also known as Snake Lily) grows to an ultimate height of five to seven feet, though the actual length of the twining stem may be twice that as it winds in, out, under, and over various chaparral shrubs on its way to the sky and light.

During the two- to four-week growth of the stem, the terminal flower bud remains dormant. Later, the bud develops into a dense cluster of fifteen to thirty tiny bright pink flowers, making a tight head similar to that of Blue Brodiaea. Though the flower head is usually two to three inches across, I have read accounts of some that were six inches wide. What a marvelous sight that must have been!

Harvest Brodiaea begins to bloom just as the fields and grasslands are drying out from the early summer heat. *B. elegans* has three to eleven reddish-purple flowers in an open umbel like Ithuriel's Spear, borne on the main stem about twelve inches tall. The flowers have a satiny sheen, provoking images of regal dress of times long past. Look for them on dry, sandy soil and in gravelly places of the open forests.

This was an important food bulb for the native Californians. Late in spring each year, when the shoots were just appearing above ground, both men and women would spend several days harvesting the bulbs with long digging sticks. The bulbs, about an inch across, were usually found six inches underground. After sorting the bulbs, they returned the smaller ones back to the earth to ensure next year's food crop. It was eaten raw, but many thought it tastier if fried or roasted. Though the bulbs were crunchy like raw potatoes, the taste was similar to chestnuts.

Often hidden in the grasses, Pretty Face blooms in May, June, or July, depending upon the elevation. An umbel of eight to ten flowers on the six-inch-tall flower stalk, the blossoms are creamy-yellow with a dark lengthwise vein down the center of each petal. Though much smaller than those of the Harvest Brodiaea, the bulbs were sometimes harvested and eaten.

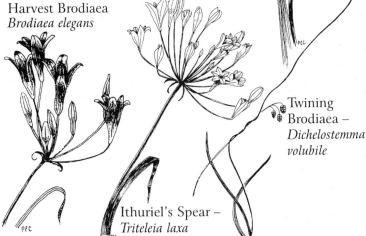

Pretty Face –
Triteleia ixioides

Harvest Brodiaea
Brodiaea elegans

Twining Brodiaea –
Dichelostemma volubile

Ithuriel's Spear –
Triteleia laxa

Turn the page to learn about Lupines, the wolf flowers. Worldwide, there are about 200 species, most of which are found in western North and South America. Of that number, over seventy species are native to California. Note the flowers, leaves, and seeds and enjoy their unique beauty.

35

A BIT ABOUT LUPINES

The genus *Lupinus* is widely distributed throughout the West. With the exception of salt marshes, it is found in all plant communities of California. Despite species differences for soil, moisture, and drainage, all Lupines have several characteristics in common: the compound leaves are palmate, the flower is pea-shaped, and the seed is enclosed in a pod resembling the garden pea or bean. The Lupine fruit, a light-brown fuzzy seed pod, twists open in half as it explodes, scattering its two to twelve seeds to faraway places.

While it's the flowers that first draw us to this beautiful plant, the leaves are equal in displaying nature's art. In the bud, the leaves are neatly folded. Upon opening, the leaves, held up by tentpole-like stems, stretch and expand into a flat plane similar to an open hand, palm up toward the sky with the leaflet fingers widely separated. Dependent upon the species, the number of leaflets varies from three to seventeen per leaf. Each leaflet, grooved lengthwise through its middle, catches raindrops or morning dew which then drains down to the center of the leaf. When the sun's rays strike that drop of water, it sparkles like a diamond—a diamond long sought after by photographers and painters alike.

The leaves of many Lupine species have a silvery color and are soft to the touch—similar to the feel of velvet or a kitten's paw. Close inspection reveals that the leaves are green, but copiously covered with fine silver hairs. According to some, the Lupine leaves follow the sun's rays—from dawn to twilight—hence one of its common names, Sundial Plant. As the day draws to a close, the leaflets fold together for the night, thereby reducing the surface area. This protects the plant from excessive chilling.

In some species, the flowers are arranged in definite rows or tiers on the stem and with almost equal spacing between each tier; in other species, they are scattered along the stem in dense clusters or spirals. With few exceptions, all five petals of the Lupine flower are of one color; variations include cream, yellow, blue-pink, purple-pink, and red-purple. The single-petalled banner stands upright in the back of the flower. Often, the banner has a conspicuous white or cream-colored spot in its center which may or may not be speckled with purplish to dark-blue dots.

The two side petals are called wings; the lower two front petals, the keels, are joined together enclosing the pistils and stamens. While searching for nectar, insects, often small bees, land on the flower. Their weight opens the keel and, like a salt shaker, the exposed stamens sprinkle pollen from their anthers onto the insects' bodies.

In Europe of the Middle Ages, farmers noticed that Lupines grew in barren soils. They believed the soil was poor because the Lupine roots took away the nutrients—as the wolf robbed them of their chickens. Therefore, these plants were given the genus name *Lupinus,* derived from the word "lupus", meaning wolf. Contrary to these farmers' beliefs, Lupines prosper in nutrient-poor sandy or rocky soils because the nitrogen-fixing nodules on their roots contain bacteria which can convert nitrogen from the air in the soil into a form usable by the plant.

Once you recognize the palmate leaves of Lupine, you'll discover these plants throughout the West—from groundhugging plants to five-foot-tall bushes. However, the species names may elude you, as there are over seventy species of Lupines in California and several of those interbreed. Both flowers and seed, as well as information about plant size and habitat, are needed to positively identify most species.

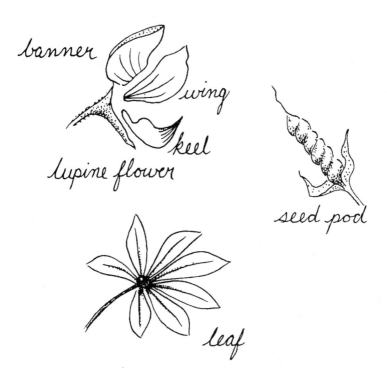

banner

wing

keel

lupine flower

seed pod

leaf

Perhaps you've come upon Lupines along the roadsides in the foothills—with pea-like flowers on a spike above the basal leaves, some creamy-white and others blue-purple to red-purple. Stop, then saunter over to the flowers to relish their exquisite colors and their fragrance.

SOME FOOTHILL LUPINES

Bush Lupine, Sky Lupine, and White Lupine, common to California, are enjoyed by thousands of people as they travel throughout the state. They can be seen growing on rocky cuts and hillsides or at roadsides, in chaparral and foothill woodlands from southern Oregon to southern California.

Of all the Lupine species indigenous to California, only Bush Lupine, *Lupinus albifrons,* is considered a shrub. From its woody base, Bush Lupine usually grows two to three feet tall, but sometimes can reach five feet. Its branches, stems, and six to ten leaflets are covered with silky hairs, lending a silvery appearance to the plant—hence another common name, Silver Lupine. Bush Lupine, an evergreen plant, sheds some of its leaves in the hot, dry days of late summer to conserve water for its survival.

It blooms from March to April in the southlands and the lower foothills, but you'll find it in blossom through June in the Sierra Nevada mountains below 5000 feet elevation. The showy flowers—variously described as intense blue-purple, magenta-purple, blue- to red-purple, reddish-purple, or violet to lavender—are displayed on twelve-inch-tall spikes. The upright back petal, the banner, has a large white or yellowish-colored spot its lower part. In addition to the visual treat that Bush Lupine offers, you'll also discover an olfactory one. When strolling past these bushes in the early afternoon, you'll catch a whiff of the wonderful, sweet perfume as it floats on the prevailing breezes.

Sky Lupine, *Lupinus nanus,* grows throughout most of California's foothills on sunny, gravelly slopes and open grasslands below 3900 feet. The leaflets, varying in number from five to nine, are narrow and about one-half to one inch long. Both sides are covered with long hairs. Sky Lupine, an annual, often branches at its base, reaching up to twenty inches in height.

The young buds on the eight- to ten-inch flower spikes are light blue, turning to a brilliant blue upon opening. When viewed from a distance, and with a fleeting glance, one might assume that Sky Lupine has both blue and white petals. However, close inspection reveals that the banner petal, low and rounded, has a prominent white spot with a yellowish base. The white spot, flecked with dark blue-purple dots, is a nectary guide for insects and adds beauty for us to enjoy. You'll easily recognize the fragrant blue carpets of Sky Lupine especially when mixed with California Poppies—the blue and gold of springtime California.

Growing from British Columbia through California to Baja, *Lupinus*

38

microcarpus var. densiflorus or White Lupine, commonly seen in the lower foothills throughout California, can occasionally be found at elevations up to 4800 feet. The five to eleven leaflets, gray-green in color, are borne on stout hollow stems, four to thirty-two inches tall. The stems are simple at the base of the plant, but nearer to the middle they divided into numerous, wide-spreading branches, each bearing leaves.

A distinctive feature of White Lupine is the arrangement of its flowers on the ten-inch stalks which rise above the foliage. The flowers are wrapped about the stem in precise tiers, five or six dense whorls per stem.

While White Lupine is the only California species of Lupine with white or cream-colored flowers, many of Nature's plants are mavericks—and this Lupine is no exception. Occasionally, you'll find *Lupinus microcarpus var. densiflorus* with bright yellow or lavender or pink flowers, neatly arranged in tiers, each of which is in dense whorls around the stem—typical of the White Lupine.

Sky Lupine –
Lupinus nanus

White Lupine –
Lupinus microcarpus
var. *densiflorus*

Bush Lupine – *Lupinus albifrons*

In the grassy foothills, already brown, it seems almost too hot for any delicate, dainty flowers to blossom. Yet seemingly fragile, Farewell-to-Spring, with its four elegant pink petals, remains perky even as the temperature rises.

CLARKIAS
(Farewell-to-Spring, Four Hearts, Elegant Clarkia, and Red Ribbons)

In late spring, the hills blush with the purplish-pink Clarkias as the grasses dry up and the formerly green slopes turn to golden-brown. These flowers seem to cheerfully announce the advent of summer with warmer weather to come. The genus was named in honor of Captain William Clark of the 1804 Lewis and Clark Expedition.

The Clarkias are annuals, native to western North America. You will find them on open slopes or banks throughout the foothills and lower mountains from 1500 to 4500 feet elevation. They grow from one to three feet high, depending upon favorable conditions as well as species' differences. The flowers close up at night and reopen the next day; each blossom lasts several days. The gray-green leaves are linear and one to two inches long.

Two distinct flower shapes emerge in the Clarkias: the four petals arranged either as an open cup-shaped flower, as seen in Farewell-to-Spring *(Clarkia amoena)* and *C. biloba*; or in a spoke- or wheel-like fashion as displayed by Elegant Clarkia *(C. unguiculata)* and Red Ribbons *(C. concinna)*. In the latter two species, the upper parts of the petals—the blades, scissored at their tips into diamond or rounded lobes—narrow into a claw at the petal's base. *Unguiculata* means having a claw or stalk-like base; *concinna* means beautiful.

The colors of the various flower parts of the Clarkias are most unbelievable. For instance, the petals of Elegant Clarkia can vary from lavender-pink to dark reddish-purple to salmon. The sepals—the bud coverings—sometimes are purple and the stamens scarlet with four red and four creamy-white anthers. A truly WILDflower whose color drives us crazy.

Though narrow at its base, the bright pink petals of Red Ribbons are deeply cleft into three lobes at its tip. With *Clarkia biloba*, the tip of each of the rosy-purple petals is divided into two heart-shaped lobes. It has no common name, but I call it Four Hearts for the petals that are attached to the stem at the base of each heart.

The Miwok tribes considered Farewell-to-Spring seeds, as well as acorns from the Black Oak, among their most prized foods. The tops of *C. biloba* and Farewell-to-Spring were broken up, tied in bundles, and places on rocks to dry. When dried, the plants were unbundled, spread out, and beaten with a stick to loosen the seeds. They also harvested seeds from the Elegant Clarkia, removed the chaff, then stored them for treats at a later date.

Red Ribbons –
Clarkia concinna

Four Hearts –
Clarkia biloba

Farewell-to-Spring –
Clarkia amoena

Elegant Clarkia –
Clarkia unguiculata

DEC

While enjoying the Clarkias, did you see a plant with bright green, strap-like leaves nearby? With its undulating leaf edges, Soap Plant soon will sprout an asparagus-like stalk, later becoming the flower stem for its transient white blossoms.

SOAP PLANT

Whenever you observe the Soap Plant, *Chlorogalum pomeridianum,* from its first leaves to flowering, you will be amazed at this unusual plant. It is found in dry open places below 5000 feet in elevation: foothills, coastal or valley plains, open coniferous forests, oak woodlands, or in brush.

From late summer to early winter, there is no sign of this plant except for the brown fibers surrounding the bulb, and only then if it is growing in shallow ground. After heavy rains in late winter, the strap-like leaves, with undulating edges, burst forth from the dormant bulb. As with all members of the Lily Family, the leaves have long veins parallel to the edges.

By mid-spring, an asparagus-like stalk shoots up from the middle of the basal leaf rosette. This leafless flower stem reaches its full height, from eight to ten feet, by late May or early June. At this point, the stalk branches widely, and openly, with many flower buds on the various branches.

It blossoms late in the day, one flower at a time. The species name, *pomeridianum,* means post-meridian—a reference to the late afternoon appearance of each new flower. The white flowers remain open in the evening, appearing to be suspended in mid-air against the black of night. Small night-flying moths, flies, and beetles are attracted to this fleeting evening flower which lasts but one night. If you have a plant in your yard, take time each afternoon to find the new flower with six recurved petals, each about one-and-one-half inches long.

The native Californians made wide use of the bulbs of Soap Plant: for making brushes, as a cleanser, in harvesting fish, as well as for food and medicine. The fibrous outer layers of the bulbs resemble the coarse hairs of a horse's tail; the fibers at the bulb base are curved while those at its top are straight. After removal from the bulb, the straight ends were tied with cordage made from strands of the nettle or milkweed stems to make a brush. Then mucilaginous glue from the cooked bulb was worked into the string to strengthen the handle. The brushes were used for removing acorn flour from the sifting tray, cleaning the winnowing baskets, applying pigment to pictographs, or as a hair brush. The bulb was also used as a cleanser. When crushed, then mixed with a little water, the mash yields a sudsy lather. This was used for cleaning clothes and baskets; it also made a fine shampoo.

The chemical in the bulbs which produces the lathering qualities, saponin, was also useful in harvesting fish. In late June, in the foothills and low mountains when the streams would wane, there were pools of water containing fish. The women would collect the bulbs of the Soap Lily, mash them into small bits, and add them to the pool. The lathery water stupefied the fish and they floated on the water's surface. They were easily scooped up in loose-meshed baskets or picked out of the water by hand. Fortunately, cooking the fish rendered the "poison" harmless.

After long baking in an earthen oven, the California natives used the bulbs for food. The young shoots, gathered in spring, were also eaten after similar roasting. It seems that the long, slow heat broke down the saponin into innocuous by-products.

The cooked bulb had medicinal properties as well. Mashed into a paste, it was used as a salve for poison oak rashes, and for poultices on skin sores. California natives had great reverence for the plants used in medicinal cures. Instead of discarding the unused portions, they would return the "used plant" to the Earth while giving thanks for its healing properties.

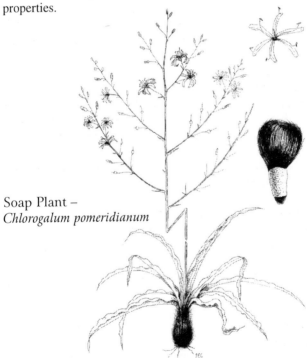

Soap Plant –
Chlorogalum pomeridianum

From fields far away, some of the flowers paint the palette with a light yellow—a color more subdued than the bright yellow of Goldfields. As you come within sight of the flowers, you realize that the largest portion of each ray petal of Tidy-tips is a bright buttery-yellow—the same as Goldfields— while the tips of the petals are white as snow.

TIDY-TIPS

Tidy-tips, *Layia platyglossa,* come into bloom in late April or early May, just as the Goldfields and Butter-and-Eggs begin to wane. Tidy-tips stands out amidst acres of other yellow blossoms. The white tips, tricking our eyes, visibly mix with the bright yellow centers, creating a creamy-yellow in the mosaic of the distant landscape. You'll find them in grasslands or inland valleys, and on open slopes of the foothills up to 4500 feet in the lower ponderosa pine forests.

Plants in the Aster or Composite Family are classified into tribes to aid in identification. Members in each tribe are closely-related genera that have several characteristics not exhibited in other tribes. Though a member of the Tarweed Tribe, Tidy-tips are definitely not as pungent as several of that tribe, but some wildflower lovers still appreciate their delicate fragrance.

An annual, Tidy-tips grow either stiffly upright or as a sprawling, many-branched plant. The height of the plant varies from four to sixteen inches, depending on its growth habit.

Tidy-tips' leaves, stems, and flower bracts are covered with short, straight hairs distinguishing it from other *Layia* species. The narrow, linear leaves are arranged alternate on the reddish-purple stems; usually the lower leaves are twice divided and the margins of the upper leaves are entire, with few or no slashes.

As is true with many Composites, Tidy-tips have both ray and disk flowers in each solitary flower head. The half-inch-long ray flowers, a bright yellow over most of their length, have white, three-lobed petal tips. The line between the white and yellow is so precise—the same distance from the tips of each of the eleven to thirteen petals—it is as if a painter used masking tape to separate the colors, or perhaps carefully dipped each tip into a bucket of white paint to a fixed depth.

The disk flowers, those in the center, are the same yellow color as that on the lower parts of the ray petals. Each disk flower has a long black stamen projecting beyond the floral tube, leaving us to imagine that the center's blossoms had been sprinkled with black pepper.

Platyglossa means "broad tongue", probably referring to the one-third-inch-wide petals. The genus was named for George Tradescant Lay, a botanist with Captain Beechey's expedition, who visited California in 1827.

Whenever I observe this flower close-up, my memories travel back to the springtime flowers of my childhood. Tidy-tips, with their neat and pleasing appearance, remind me of a little girl, in a crisp, white, starched pinafore worn over a buttery-yellow organdy dress, skipping through the hills of daffodils in her black patent-leather Mary Janes.

Viewed up close, Tidy-tips can be mistaken for no other wildflower.

Tidy-tips – *Layia platyglossa*

Moving up in the mountains to at least 5000 feet elevation, peruse the dry wooded slopes or openings in the forest for bright yellow, sunflower-like blooms. As you approach, you soon learn that the huge woolly leaves indeed remind one of long, soft Mountain Mules Ears.

MOUNTAIN MULES EARS and CARSON PASS WILDFLOWERS

The wildflower displays in the high mountain meadows usually come to a peak in late July. At that elevation, spring is ending and early summer is on its way. One of the most spectacular areas for viewing mountain wildflowers is the Carson Pass area because of the hundreds of genus/species, the numbers of each species, and the close proximity to a good road—State Highway 88.

From Carson Pass, at 8573 feet in elevation, you hike about one-mile-and-one-quarter to one of the largest and most extraordinary wildflower gardens in the Sierra mountains. Relatively speaking, the trail is easy, meandering up and down and about with most of it barely below timberline—9000 to 10000 feet. You can see for miles, provided you can take your eyes off the myriads of flowers at your feet. I've seen many a dedicated flower-lover—cane in hand—as well as very young children, successfully reach the Garden located between Frog Lake and Winnemucca Lake.

You may decide to make a loop: starting at the Carson Pass trailhead, hike the two miles to Winnemucca Lake, then, moving past acres of Paintbrush, skip down the one-and-one-half miles to Wood's Lake. At this lake, you'll encounter flowers, not seen earlier, that adore the damp, shady woods there. Find a friend to shuttle the cars so you don't have to walk the two miles back up to the pass along the busy highway.

A plant list of the Carson Pass area notes over 250 colorful, flowering plants, in addition to forty plus species of conifers, sedges, ferns, rushes, and grasses. Of course, don't expect to see the whole 300 at one time. But you can be assured, if you go there from late July to mid-August, there will be a wide variety of blooming plants as well as hundreds of some species. Among others, you might see Paintbrush—magenta, red, orange, yellow, cream, white, green, and many hues in between—or Jacob's Ladder, Skyrocket, Lewisia, Penstemon, Pussy Paws, Columbine, Lupines, Monkeyflowers, Sulfur Flower, Larkspur, Buttercups, Rock Fringe, Phlox, Western Blue Flag, Sierra Onion, Elephant's Head, the Giant Green Gentian, and many Lilies and Mints.

The remaining wildflower discoveries in this book will be those plants that prefer to live in the higher mountains, starting with Mountain Mules Ears. Also a member of the Aster Family, *Wyethia mollis* is one of a few of the yellow-flowering Composites that is easily identified—because of its large leaves and one-and-a-half-inch-wide yellow flower heads

46

resembling small sunflowers, with yellow, rather than dark, centers.

The leaf stems of Mountain Mules Ears, one to three feet high, arise from thick, aromatic tubers. The huge leaves, eight to sixteen inches long, are densely covered with white hairs, giving them a woolly, gray appearance. With a bit of imagination, one can see that the soft, long, vertical-borne leaves, rising above the ground, do resemble the ears of an aging mule.

You'll find this perennial on dry slopes or in rocky openings of the ponderosa pine forest on up to timberline. In some gravelly soils, you can see acres of these bright yellow petals waving in the wind.

California natives ate the young shoots in spring after removing the deep, wine-colored wrappings. In autumn, they gathered the seeds in great quantities, then pounded them into a flour which was mixed with that from other seeds to make pinole. Medicinally, for fever patients, a decoction—an aqueous extract—was used as a sponge bath, causing the person to sweat profusely and thereby "break" the fever. This decoction was not taken internally as it was poisonous.

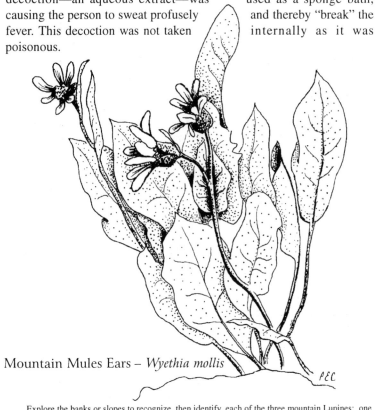

Mountain Mules Ears – *Wyethia mollis*

Explore the banks or slopes to recognize, then identify, each of the three mountain Lupines: one with pink, yellow, and white flowers; another, a tall plant bathing its feet in marshy meadows; and the last, a rock-lover at timberline with silvery, moss-like foliage.

MOUNTAIN LUPINES

Assuming you are at the proper elevations, you will easily recognize these mountain dwellers: Harlequin Lupine, *Lupinus stiversii,* usually found above 3000 feet up to 6300 feet; Many-leaved or Meadow Lupine, *Lupinus polyphyllus,* from 4000 to 9000 feet; and, Brewer's Lupine, *Lupinus breweri,* from 4000 to 12000 feet elevation.

Of these three, Harlequin or Clown Lupine dips down to the lowest elevation. At times, you might find it at 2000 feet in well-drained, sandy, or rocky places of the oak woodlands or chaparral, though it grows larger and more profusely at higher elevations in the mixed evergreen forests. Harlequin Lupine ranges from the western slopes of the Sierra to the mountains of southern California.

This succulent-appearing plant may reach twenty inches, though it is more commonly eight to ten inches tall. The leaf stems, one to three inches long, branch from the main stem. The bright green leaves are divided into leaflets, usually seven.

The flower head, in a one- to three-inch terminal spike, is short, blunt, and dense; the flowers are not whorled around the stem. However, the unique colors of its flowers draw us to this plant—and set it apart from other Lupines. Blooming from April to July, the buds are yellow and the flowers, upon opening, have spectacular spring colors: the wings are a clear, bright rose-pink, the banner is yellow and, as it ages, changes to an even brighter shade of yellow-orange. The two keel petals folded together are white, tipped with purple. If only we could grow this annual in our backyards!

Meadow or Many-leaved Lupine, unlike most Lupines, prefers to have its feet wet, enjoying the acidic soils of bogs, marshes, or meadows from southeastern Alaska, down through Washington, Oregon, and California, then east to Colorado and Montana. In California, it can be found in mountain meadows of the ponderosa pine forest up to the red fir forests.

Extravagance best describes Meadow Lupine. As the tallest Lupine in California, this perennial reaches up to six feet, its many leaves are large—up to six inches across—and each lush, light-green leaf has five to seventeen leaflets.

The fragrant, half-inch flowers, arranged in dense whorls, bloom first at the base of the six- to sixteen-inch flower spike. The bottom rows have many flowers and, with decreasing numbers up the stalk, the top rows have very few. Each flower spike with thirty or more blossoms rises above the foliage in a tall, narrow tower, more or less triangular in shape. Blooming from June to August, the flower color varies from violet to lavender to pink to white, though a rich blue-purple is the color most often seen. The banner petal has a yellow or white patch, which sometimes turns to red-purple. Meadow Lupine, one of the largest, most lush, and beautiful Lupines, is worth the trek up to the mountain meadows to indulge.

The highest mountain dweller, *Brewer's Lupine* grows from the ponderosa pine forest up to the treeless alpine region. Like the Harlequin Lupine, it prefers sandy, gravelly, or rocky slopes in openings of the coniferous forests. Only two to twelve inches tall, this woody perennial is matted or tufted, extending its two- to four-inch stiff branches out from its base. Above timberline, where the conditions are most harsh, Brewer's Lupine hugs the rocks, sometimes barely more than an inch or so tall.

The gray-green leaves are clustered near the base of the plant, with the five to ten shaggy-haired leaflets less than an inch long. When not in bloom, Brewer's Lupine looks like frosted silver moss. From June to August, Brewer's Lupine forms a tight cluster of flowers up to two inches long, each individual flower about one-fourth inch and—to match the alpine sky—a pure blue or lavender-blue with a broad white spot on the banner petal.

Harlequin Lupine –
Lupinus stiversii

Meadow Lupine –
Lupinus polyphyllus

Brewer's Lupine – *Lupinus breweri*

In damp meadows and near creeks, get a glimpse of a lacy-leaved plant with red and yellow flowers dancing at the stem's end. Like a river, the yellow of the stamens flows out of the Columbine flower as it falls over the lips of the petals.

COLUMBINE

The Columbine, *Aquilegia formosa,* is a delight to behold with its variously-lobed, thin, light green, lacy leaves and its scarlet and yellow nodding flowers. One must wander through moist montane forests and meadows to see these unusual flowers.

Gently lift the blossom and look into it. You will see the open yellow throats of the five scarlet-red tubular petals, the five sepals behind the tubes, and long bunches of yellow stamens, reaching well beyond the petals' edges.

In most flowers, the sepals are green and, after the flower opens, they usually form a ring underneath the flower—the calyx. However, the sepals of this incomparable flower are scarlet-red and flare out behind the petal tubes—rather than hiding beneath the petals.

The petals of the Columbine flowers are unusually long, ending in scarlet spurs—a tubular extension of the petals with special honey glands at the end of the blunt spur. (These glands exude droplets of nectar for favored pollinators.) The shape and proportions of the spurs, topped with the honey glands, might remind some imaginative persons of doves in a circle, socializing, or maybe waiting for a drink. This scene may account for the origin of the flower's common name, Columbine, derived from "columba", Latin for dove.

As long-tongued butterflies and bumblebees or hummingbirds gather the deeply-hidden nectar, they brush against the stamens and collect pollen on their bodies which will be deposited inside the next flower they visit. However, not all visitors to the flower collect pollen. Honey bees or small beetles, from time to time, cut or bite open the tip of the honey gland from the outside and steal the sweets without pollinating the flower. Could the reason that the stamens are so long and extend past the petals' lips be that they provide insurance against failed pollination?

The derivation of the genus name, *Aquilegia,* is unclear although the species name is apparent—*formosa* means "beautiful". Some say *Aquilegia* is derived from "aquila", Latin for eagle, as the petal spurs suggest claws. Yet others maintain it is derived from the Latin word, "aquilegus", meaning "water-drawer", which would reflect the moist habitat that Columbine plants prefer.

So choose the meaning you like: doves and eagles, or doves near the water. But, can you imagine doves and eagles on the same flower?

PEC

Columbine – *Aquilegia formosa*

If you leave the creeks and wend your way to drier rocky areas that have recently been cleared or burned, you might lay your eyes on a single, woolly-white plant, growing several feet from any of its kin. Perhaps the chemicals in its leaves, distinctly fragrant, protect each Pearly Everlasting from its relatives.

PEARLY EVERLASTING

From the Atlantic to the Pacific, in the upper parts of the North American continent, dipping down into the Rockies, then to Monterey, California, up to Alaska and across the Bering Strait to northeastern Asia, Pearly Everlasting grows in areas where the soil has been disturbed along roadsides, in logging clear cuts, burned fields, or rocky areas. In the Sierra, you'll also find it on the rocky margins of meadows below 8500 feet elevation. This was one of the first plants to return to Mount Saint Helens as Earth recovered from the May 1980 volcanic eruption—a true pioneer.

Pearly Everlasting, *Anaphalis margaritacea,* belongs to the Everlasting Tribe in the Aster or Composite Family. Members of this tribe have no ray florets and all the plants have woolly stems, leaves, and flower heads. The term, everlasting, refers to the flower's keeping qualities. When the flowers are picked before they are fully opened, then hung upside down in a cool, well-ventilated place, they will retain their color and texture for many months after drying.

Pearly Everlasting, a solitary plant growing several feet away from any other of its kind, spreads by underground runners which send up new shoots each spring. It's a perennial that rises to two feet, with leaves arranged alternate as they proceed up the unbranched stalk; the almost white plants are appealing in spring and summer.

The leaves are one to four inches long and sometimes curled under, toward their woolly undersides. The upper surfaces of the new leaves have silvery hairs giving the leaf a light gray look. Later, the hairs fall off and the leaves "green" with age.

The one-fourth- to one-half-inch flowers, contained in an oval-shaped flower head up to two-and-a-half inches wide, bloom from June to August. The flowers are dioecious: the male plants bear clusters of yellow florets each with several anthers; the female plants look similar but have two stigmas, and no anthers.

Each of the disk florets is surrounded by several rows of parchment-like bracts or scales, arranged in a shingle-like pattern. Pearly-white in appearance, these bracts resemble sharp-pointed ray florets. Before the florets are fully opened, they remind one of small pearls, hence the species name, *margaritacea,* meaning pearl.

The silvery hairs and the large amounts of tannin in the leaves protect the plant from sucking insects such as aphids. However, the American Painted Butterfly rears its caterpillars on these leaves and its pupae builds nests using the hairs.

With its everlasting properties and insecticidal qualities, this wildflower intrigued the European explorers. Because they brought it back with them to the Old World in the sixteenth century, today's Europeans could easily think it a native. Pearly Everlasting was one of thirty to forty American plant species which appeared in a catalog of garden plants published in England in 1656.

According to some, it was growing "plentifully" in English gardens by 1674. Various parts of this plant were often used as a cure for coughs, colds, head pain, bruises, strains, or worms.

In my research, I was disappointed not to find mention, except for its use as an insecticide, of the fragrance, odor, or pungency of Pearly Everlasting. My illustrator says it smells of maple syrup; to this writer, of wonderful curry. Check it out and see how it teases your nose.

Pearly Everlasting –
Anaphalis margaritacea

PEC

While hiking up past the montane forest into sunny places, you may get a whiff of mint as you pass some flowers with purple-blue heads. If the leaves are opposite, you have met up with a member of the Mint Family—in this case, Mountain Pennyroyal.

MOUNTAIN PENNYROYAL

The genus name, *Monardella,* meaning little *Monarda,* was given in honor of Nicolas Bautista Monardes who was born the year after Columbus came to the Americas. Monardes was an expert botanist and a well-known and widely-read Spanish physician of the sixteenth century. He studied American plants at the docks of Seville and later published the first book on the flora of the Americas which was translated into English under the title, *Joyfull Newes out of the New Founde World.* He had a large business investment, importing plants from the New World that he used for pharmacological purposes. Pennyroyal, the common name, is derived from the French words, "pulial royal"—the plant was used as the royal remedy against fleas.

Monardella odoratissima, one of the spiciest flowers in alpine gardens, grows from the ponderosa pine forest at 3000 feet up to 11000 feet elevation. Like so many of the high mountain dwellers, this branched perennial, somewhat woody at its base, prefers gravelly flats, dry slopes, ridges, and open forest floors.

The aromatic leaves are arranged opposite on the stems, a characteristic common to all members of the Mint Family. At higher altitudes, you need not crush the leaves to smell the delicious minty odor of Pennyroyal—gentle breezes will bring you wafts from nearby blossoms.

One to several flower stems arise from the basal mat of gray-green foliage. The flower head is especially attractive before blooming when the round, purple-tinted buds are held high above the ground. Each of the stems, leafy and hairy, and about six to twelve inches long, are topped with a pincushion of lavender-blue flowers, the cluster almost an inch in diameter. When Pennyroyal blooms from June to September, bees and butterflies visit the flowers by day; the hummingbird moths appear at dusk to sip the nectar of the lighter-colored lavender flowers.

Many consider Pennyroyal tea among the best of all herbal drinks— a single stem plus the attached flowers is enough herbage to make a couple of cups of tea, minty in taste and smell. The aromatic leaves from older plants likewise make a refreshing beverage.

California natives ate the leaves and stalks in spring and made a thirst-quenching drink of the leaves and stems. Additionally, they used the tea for colds and fevers, and colic; others thought it purified the blood. Sometimes the early settlers drank the tea to treat colds and hay fever.

As for Dr. Monardes, he must have been practicing excellent personal medicine, for he lived to be ninety-five years old—only twelve years short of 1700. Incidentally, Bee Balm, a *Monarda* species, is another delightful member of the aromatic Mint Family.

Mountain Pennyroyal – *Monardella odoratissima*

You may run across a plant in sunny, gravelly, or sandy spots with umbrella-like spokes, each about six inches long. Touch the clusters of pink flowers at the ends of the spokes and feel the softness of a kitten's paw.

PUSSY PAWS

A ground-hugging perennial, *Calyptridium umbellatum* starts life each year from a taproot which produces a circle of leaves, the latter on short slender stems. The genus name, *Calyptridium,* from the Greek word, "kaluptra", meaning cap or cover, describes the way the petals close over the seed capsule with age. The species name refers to the umbrella-like spokes of the flower stems. Though a member of the Portulaca Family, Pussy Paws is often mistaken for Buckwheat because the leaves of each are arranged in basal rosettes and the flowers of both plants are tightly clumped into fuzzy-looking pompoms.

You'll find Pussy Paws growing on sandy or rocky soils from the ponderosa pine forest at 3000 feet on up to tree-line. This western wildflower ranges from British Columbia down through the Sierra to Baja and then east to Utah, Wyoming, and Montana.

The leaves of Pussy Paws are thin and leathery, in contrast with the fleshy leaves of other members of this family such as Red Maids, Bitter Root, and Portulaca. They are bright green, spoon-shaped, and up to two-and-a-half inches long.

The wine-red flower stems, two to ten in number, radiate from the center of the plant; they may be one to three inches long at high elevation, up to six or eight inches long at lower elevations. In any event, the stems always extend several inches beyond the outer perimeter of the leaf rosette.

The flower clusters at the end of the stems are one-half inch or more in diameter. The clusters on each stem grow in bunches and look much like the pink cushions on the underpaw of a kitten. If you gently hold one of the "paws" in your hand, you'll feel how the common name of this plant originated.

Each flower has two broad sepals, up to one-fourth inch long, and four shorter petals. The tiny petals are white and inconspicuous; it's the papery sepals, commonly tinged a pale pink to a vibrant deep rose-purple, that make the flower heads colorful and attractive. As the blossoms vanish, each flower leaves behind a tiny seed enclosed in a papery wing. When the sepals dry up and fall off, the earth around the plant becomes white from the wing flakes. The seeds are greedily gobbled up by chipmunks and other small rodents; in this process, some seeds will be dispersed to new locations.

Pussy Paws thrive in a hot, dry environment because the plant through evolution has developed a system to cool itself off. In the late evening or early morning hours, when the temperature is cooler, the flowers lie almost flat on the ground. In the middle of the day as the soil and air heat up, the flower stems become more rigid and tense. As a result of the increased water pressure in the cells of the stems, the flower clusters are lifted several inches off the hot ground. As the day wanes, and a cooler temperature returns, the clusters drop down and again rest on the earth.

Small children love this diminutive plant, squatting down to smell the flowers and to pet the soft paws as though it were a favorite furry animal. I admire the tenacity of this plant to live and blossom, and I, too, love to stroke it. It's a touch of velvet in an otherwise harsh environment.

Pussy Paws – *Calyptridium umbellatum*

Walking along in the sunny areas of the gritty, sandy mountain soil, you spy a hummingbird enjoying the nectar from a bright red tubular flower. With its petal tips folded back, Skyrocket reminds one of Fourth of July fireworks.

SKYROCKET

As if poised for blast-off, each flower of Skyrocket stands out horizontally from its stem. From the base of the slender corolla tube, the five petals flare out like fireworks—seemingly folded back at right angles to make the petal top flat. This gives the appearance of a spent rocket, hence the common name.

At one time, the genus name was *Gilia,* honoring an eighteenth century Spanish botanist, Felipe Gil. This probably accounts for one common name, Scarlet Gilia. Now the genus name is *Ipomopsis* which means "of striking appearance"; the species, *aggregata* meaning "flocking together".

Skyrocket was discovered in 1806 in Idaho by members of the Lewis and Clark Expedition. A true westerner, it ranges from British Columbia to Montana, Idaho, eastern Oregon, then to southern California. A mountain dweller, you'll find it from 3500 to 10000 feet, preferring the dry slopes and rocky ridges of the foothills on up to montane clearings, thriving on gravelly or sandy soils. Skyrocket shares the thin air of mountain slopes with other members of its Phlox Family: Spreading Phlox and two *Polemonium* species, Sky Pilot and Jacob's Ladder.

Some say this plant is a perennial because it may live for three to six years. However, horticulturally speaking, Skyrocket is more accurately described as a biennial—producing a low rosette of feathery foliage atop a taproot the first year; blooming, setting seed, and dying down the second year. Sometimes, it doesn't bloom and set seed that second year and, until it does, it continues to live from year to year like a non-blooming perennial.

The dark green, one- to two-inch, finely dissected leaves give off an unusual odor, especially when covered with moisture, reminding some of a certain black and white furry mammal. This helps to explain two other common names: Skunk Flower and Polecat Plant. Though the smell was not pleasant, my nasal investigation of some crushed leaves did not corroborate the presence of a skunk-like odor.

Blooming from May to September, the one- to one-and-a-half-inch trumpet-shaped flowers are borne in the upper leaf axils and in clusters near the top of the stem—often on one side of the stem. There are usually four to six blossoms per plant, but sometimes as many as fifteen. The color varies greatly, from an intense scarlet-red to hot pink to nearly white. The red flowers are mottled with yellow, the pink ones with white dots.

It is a hummingbird flower, as suggested by its long stigma and stamens which extend well beyond the lips of the bright red petals.

Skyrocket is also visited by hawkmoths, white-line sphinx moths, beeflies, and long- and short-tongued bees. From late afternoon into the night, the moths feed on the lighter pink or white flowers which stand out in the darkness. The bees and beeflies resort to biting open the bottom of the flower tube from the outside, to reach the nectar, since their proboscides are too short to drink from inside the flower.

The native Californians did not use *Ipomopsis* for food, though it had medicinal uses: an aqueous extract served as a blood tonic, disinfectant, and eye wash. A tea, made from the leaves, was drunk to relieve stomach aches. Some tribes made a blue dye from the roots and a glue by boiling the whole plant in water.

Skyrocket – *Ipomopsis aggregata*

In rocky crevices or cracks, not too far from Skyrockets, you'll discover sulfur-yellow flowers blooming in a rounded compact clump—sometimes two to three feet across. Examine the clusters of tiny blossoms of Sulfur Flower held on stems that are arranged in an umbrella-like fashion above its leaves.

SULFUR FLOWER

Far showier and larger than many of the California Buckwheats, *Eriogonum umbellatum* is commonly found in dry open places below 11000 feet elevation. In the mountains of Washington, Oregon, California, and the Rockies, Sulfur Flower often grows in crevices of boulders or cracks in rocky walls where it seems almost impossible for a plant to subsist. However, by choosing inhospitable places where few other plants abide, the Buckwheats' chances for survival are greatly increased.

The origin of the genus name, *Eriogonum,* is from the Greeks: "erion", meaning wool, and "gonu", knee or joint—a reference to the hairy nodes of some species.

The growth habit of this perennial is most variable. Often a low, scraggly, sprawling plant, it may reach a height of only four inches and a width of twelve inches. Yet, in other places you will find plants with erect stems up to two feet tall, spreading out about three feet. The leaves, spatula-shaped, occur both in the basal rosettes and as whorls at main branching points of the stems. The long-stemmed gray-green leaves have woolly undersides.

Likewise, the flowers of Sulfur Flower do not fit a simple mold. Blooming from July to September, the umbrella-like flower heads at the end of the foot-high flower stems are held in rounded clusters, each two to four inches wide. Some plants have as many as twenty to thirty flower clusters—so many as to hide the leaves, thereby creating a freestanding half-sphere of yellow.

Entirely lacking petals, each of the quarter-inch flowers has six brightly colored sepals which vary in color from light lemon yellow to bright yellow to a green-tinged yellow. Additionally, flowers on some plants may be speckled with bright red, adding bright hues to the landscape and contrasting sharply with the grayish-white granite.

Shoots and leaves of *Eriogonum* were eaten in the spring by California natives; in the fall, they gathered seeds of several species of Buckwheat, then ground it into flour. Tea was made from the roots, flowers, or leaves of Sulfur Flower to treat headaches and stomach problems; and it was also used as a general blood tonic, a cure for colds and coughs as well as a treatment for dermatitis. From time to time, ears were pierced using the hardwood from Buckwheat twigs.

Sulfur Flower – *Eriogonum umbellatum*

In the lower growing range for the Sulfur Flower, between 5000 and 6000 feet elevation, have you ever stumbled upon a three- to six-foot bulbous plant with several whorls of bright green leaves? Take in the spicy fragrance of the white Washington Lily—a most sensuous and unforgettable moment.

WASHINGTON LILY

Called the Queen of the Lilies by some, Washington Lily was a favorite of John Muir, naturalist and mountain man, who walked through acres of wildflowers while hiking all over California more than one hundred twenty-five years ago.

Early European settlers in California called this Lily, the Lady Washington Lily, after the first First Lady. Dr. Albert Kellogg, an early California botanist, decided to break the rules of taxonomic nomenclature to name the species, *"washingtonianum"*, honoring the settlers' common name. The genus name, *Lilium,* is derived from "leiron", a classical Greek word for lily—their word for purity. The lily became the Greek symbol for purity because of the pure white color of some.

One of only a few native Lilies that prefer a dry environment, you'll see it on steep, well-drained slopes in forest openings or amidst montane chaparral between the elevations of 4000 and 7000 feet. This Lily ranges from northern Oregon, to the mountains of northern California, then down the Sierra Nevada mountains. It seems to haunt areas of low shrubbery which offer cover and protection during its leaf growth and flowering.

When the leaves first emerge, their greatest threat is from squirrels or chipmunks; each animal sits erect, clasps the stems, and chomps away, feasting on the foliage. If the leaves survive the smaller rascals, you will be most fortunate to see the blossoms later, as deer not only relish the remaining foliage, but devour the two- to three-inch-long flower buds. In spite of all these growing hardships, I have seen Washington Lilies in the wilds that reached heights of eight to ten feet—in full bloom. Usually they are only four to six feet tall.

The shiny, light green leaves are arranged in whorls at intervals—as many as nine—along the stalk. At each whorl, the one- to four-inch-long leaves stand out horizontally from the stalk. Every time I take a fleeting glance at the foliage, I am reminded of a clown collar, green and ruffled, hugging a very thin neck.

The Washington Lily blooms from June to August, depending upon the elevation. The snowy-white flowers can be large—up to five inches across—and dotted with tiny reddish-purple spots inside. Each stalk may have twenty or more of the trumpet-shaped flowers blooming at its top. The flower is intensely fragrant which attracts nectar-loving ants in the daytime and moths in the evening

And so, with the discovery of this deliciously fragrant Lily, our book comes to a close. Remain intimate with the wildflowers as you continue to pursue them, for you might find numerous cousins of those you already know. Until the next book appears, enjoy each and every wildflower while sharing your newfound knowledge with friends and relatives.

Washington Lily – *Lilium washingtonianum*

GLOSSARY

Annual. A plant that germinates, blooms, sets seed, and dies in one growing season.

Anthers. The pollen-producing parts of the flower situated at the top of the stamens, the male reproductive organs.

Basal. At or near the base of a plant or other plant parts.

Banner. The upright petal at the back of the Pea or Legume flower.

Biennial. A plant that completes its life cycle in two growing seasons, usually flowering only in the second year.

Bract. A modified leaf arising below the solitary flower or the inflorescence.

Coniferous. Cone-bearing plants, mostly evergreen, with needles or scale-like leaves.

Decoction. The solution containing the flavor or essence of plants that is extracted by boiling various plant parts in water.

Dioecious. Genera which have their reproductive parts, stamens and pistils, on separate plants. (See Pearly Everlasting.)

Endemic. Indigenous; originating in and characterizing a particular region.

Family. A broad group of plants, usually consisting of several genera, which have similar characteristics based on flower and fruit structures.

Fruit. The dry or fleshy capsule or pod that contains the mature seeds of a plant.

Genus. The first subdivision of plants in a family that contains related species; the first part of a plant's botanical name.

Genera. Plural of genus.

Habitat. The total environment of a plant that supports its specific needs: soil, water, temperature, light, elevation, companion plants.

Hemiparasite. A parasite, possessing chlorophyll, that invades its host to obtain only mineral nutrients and water.

Honey glands. Special glands at the base of the petals, pistil, and stamens that exude droplets of nectar.

Inflorescence. The entire cluster of flowers on the main flower stem arranged either as heads, unbels, racemes, or panicles.

Keel. The two fused petals, enclosing the stamens and pistil, located at the base of the Pea or Legume flower.

Mary Janes. Flat dress shoes with a one-button strap, often made of patent leather.

Montane. Pertaining to mountain environments, usually at or below timberline.

Muir, John. A nineteenth-century Scottish naturalist who came to California in the late 1860s to study its fauna and flora.

Native Californians. The indigenous people of California who lived here thousands of years before the arrival of the Europeans.

Nectar. A sugary fluid secreted in some flowers to entice animal pollinators.

Nectary. See Honey glands.

Organdy. A fine, thin cotton fabric usually stiff and having a crisp finish; used in the early 1900s.

Pedicel. The stalk of an individual flower in an inflorescence.

Peduncle. The main flower stalk of an entire inflorescence or of a solitary flower.

Perennial. A plant living through more than two growing seasons.

Petals. The showy, colored parts of a flower, though sometimes bracts or sepals take over that function.

Petals, irregular-shaped. Two or more petal sizes and shapes, non-symmetrical in arrangement.

Petals, regular-shaped. All petals of the same size and shape and arranged symmetrically.

Petiole. The stalk that attaches a leaf to the stem.

Pinafore. A child's apron usually large enough to cover most of a dress.

Pinole. A meal or flour made from small seeds which were parched and then pulverized; sometimes the meal was pressed into cakes.

Pollen. Fine, dust-like substance found in the anthers; each grain contains two cells which divide to form the male sperm cells.

Pollination. The process whereby the pollen from the anthers is deposited on the stigma, the uppermost part of the pistil.

Pubescence. Short hairs on the leaf's surface that give it a downy feel and offer protection against plant-eating insects.

Recurved. Flower petals, and sometimes sepals, which turn back on themselves. (See Washington Lily.)

Reflexed. Petals which are sharply recurved. (See Shooting Stars.)

Scape. A leafless flowering stalk often arising from a cluster of basal leaves. (See Shooting Stars.)

Sepals. The outer whorl of a flower that protects the flower bud; usually green in color, though sometimes brightly colored. (See Columbine.)

Species. A division of members of a genus into groups of plants that share several common characteristics and also interbreed freely; the second part of a plant's botanical name.

Spur. A tubular extension of the petals or sepals that contains the nectar. (See Columbine.)

Trumpet. A flower with regular-shaped petals that are united to form a tube.

Two-lipped flowers. Flowers with irregular-shaped petals whose upper petals are usually turned back and whose lower petals are turned down. (See Common Monkeyflower, Chinese Houses, and Butter-and-Eggs.)

Umbel. A head of flowers whose stems branch out from the end of the main flower stem in an umbrella- or spoke-like fashion.

Wings. The two side petals of the Pea or Legume flower.

SELECTED BIBLIOGRAPHY

Art, Henry W., *The Wildflower Gardener's Guide, Pacific Northwest, Rocky Mountain, and Western Canada Edition.* Pownal, VT. Storey Communications, Inc., 1990.

Barbour, Michael, Bruce Pavlik, Frank Drysdale, and Susan Lindstrom, *California's Changing Landscapes: Diversity and Conservation of California Vegetation.* Sacramento, CA. The California Native Plant Society, 1993.

Barrett, Samuel A. and Edward W. Gifford, *Miwok Material Culture: Indian Life of the Yosemite Region.* Bulletin of Milwaukee Public Museum, Vol. 2, No. 4. Yosemite National Park, CA. Yosemite Association, 1933.

Carville, Julie Stauffer, *Lingering in Tahoe's Wild Gardens.* Chicago Park, CA. Mountain Gypsy Press, 1989.

Clements, Edith C., "Wild Flowers of the West", *The National Geographic Magazine,* Vol. LI (May, 1927), 566-622.

Coats, Alice M., *The Plant Hunters.* New York, NY. McGraw-Hill Book Company, 1969.

Coffey, Timothy, *The History and Folklore of North American Wildflowers.* New York, NY. Houghton Mifflin Company, 1993.

Crittenden, Mabel, *Wildflowers of the West.* Blaine, WA. Hancock House Publishers, 1992.

Dale, Nancy, *Flowering Plants, the Santa Monica Mountains, Coastal and Chaparral Regions of Southern California.* Santa Barbara, CA. Capra Press, 1986.

Hall, Clarence A., Jr., Editor, *Natural History of the White-Inyo Range Eastern California,* California Natural History Guide: 55. Berkeley, CA. University of California Press, 1991.

Haskin, Leslie L., *Wild Flowers of the Pacific Coast.* Portland, OR. Metropolitan Press, 1934.

Hickman, James C., Editor, *The Jepson Manual: Higher Plants of California.* Berkeley, CA. University of California Press, 1993.

Houk, Rose, *Wildflowers of the American West.* San Francisco, CA. Chronicle Books, 1987.

Jepson, Willis Linn, *A Manual of the Flowering Plants of California.* Berkeley, CA. University of California Press, 1925.

Keator, Glenn, *Complete Guide to the Native Perennials of California.* San Francisco, CA. Chronicle Books, 1990.

——, *Plants of the East Bay Parks.* Niwot, CO. Roberts Rinehart Publishers, Inc., 1994.

Lenz, Lee W., *Native Plants for California Gardens.* Claremont, CA. Rancho Santa Ana Botanic Garden, 1956.

Mighetto, Lisa, Editor, "The Bee-Pastures of California." In *Muir Among the Animals.* San Francisco, CA. Sierra Club Books, 1986.

Morgenson, Dana C., *Yosemite Wildflower Trails.* El Portal, CA. Yosemite Natural History Association, 1975.

Munz, Philip A., *California Mountain Wildflowers*. Berkeley, CA. University of California Press, 1963.

——, *California Spring Wildflowers*. Berkeley, CA. University of California Press, 1961.

—— and David D. Keck, *A California Flora*. Berkeley, CA. University of California Press, 1959.

Niehaus, Theodore F., *A Field Guide to Pacific States Wildflowers,* The Peterson Guide Series. Boston, MA. Houghton Mifflin Company, 1976.

Parsons, Mary Elizabeth, *The Wild Flowers of California*. San Francisco, CA. Cunningham, Curtiss & Welch, 1909.

Rowntree, Lester, *Hardy Californians*. Salt Lake City, UT. Peregrine Smith, Inc., 1980.

Schmidt, Marjorie G., *Growing California Native Plants,* California Natural History Guides. Berkeley, CA. University of California Press, 1980.

Spellenberg, Richard, *The Audubon Society Field Guide to North American Wildflowers: Western Region*. New York, NY. Alfred A. Knopf, Inc., 1979.

Stokes, Donald W. and Lillian Q., *The Wildflower Book: From the Rockies West*. Boston, MA. Little, Brown and Company, 1993.

Storer, Tracy I. and Robert L. Usinger, *Sierra Nevada Natural History*. Berkeley, CA. University of California Press, 1963.

Strike, Sandra S., *Ethnobotany of the California Indians. Vol. 2: Aboriginal Uses of California's Indigenous Plants*. Champaign, IL. Koeltz Scientific Books USA, 1994.

Weeden, Norman F., *A Sierra Nevada Flora*. Berkeley, CA. Wilderness Press, 1996.

Whitney, Stephen, *Western Forests*. National Audubon Society Nature Guides. New York, NY. Alfred A. Knopf, Inc., 1985.

Wilson, Jim and Lynn, and Jeff Nicholas, *Wildflowers of Yosemite*. El Portal, CA. Sierra Press, Inc., 1987.

Ulrich, Larry, *Wildflowers of California*. Santa Barbara, CA. Companion Press, 1995.

INDEX OF PLANT NAMES